OCCASIONAL PAPER 165

Algeria: Stabilization and Transition to the Market

Karim Nashashibi, Patricia Alonso-Gamo, Stefania Bazzoni, Alain Féler, Nicole Laframboise, and Sebastian Paris Horvitz

INTERNATIONAL MONETARY FUND
Washington DC
1998

© 1998 International Monetary Fund

Production: IMF Graphics Section
Figures: Phil Torsani
Typesetting: Alicia Etchebarne-Bourdin

Cataloging-in-Publication Data

Algeria: stabilization and transition to the market / Karim Nashashibi . . . [et al.]—Washington, DC: International Monetary Fund, 1998.

    p. cm.—(Occasional paper ; ISSN 0251-6365 ; 165)

ISBN 1-55775-691-0

   1. Algeria—Economic conditions—1962. 2. Economic stabilization—Algeria. 3. Structural adjustment (Economic policy)—Algeria. 4. Monetary policy—Algeria. I. Nashashibi, Karim A. II. International Monetary Fund. III. Series: Occasional paper (International Monetary Fund); no. 165.

HC815.A44 1998

Price: US$18.00
(US$15.00 to full-time faculty members and
students at universities and colleges)

Please send orders to:
International Monetary Fund, Publication Services
700 19th Street, N.W., Washington, D.C. 20431, U.S.A.
Tel.: (202) 623-7430   Telefax: (202) 623-7201
E-mail: publications@imf.org
Internet: http://www.imf.org

recycled paper

Contents

Preface		vii
I	**Overview**	1
II	**The Setting of Economic Reform**	2
	Geographical, Historical, and Political Background	2
	The Prereform Economic System	3
	Reverse Oil Shock of 1986 and First Attempts at Reform	4
	Policy Reversal of 1992–93	7
III	**Macroeconomic Stabilization and Structural Reforms Since 1994**	8
	Objectives and Economic Policy Strategy	8
	Realignment of Relative Prices and External Trade Liberalization	8
	Macroeconomic Policies and Performance	14
	Structural and Institutional Reforms	15
IV	**Fiscal Policy**	17
	Attempts at Fiscal Adjustment Prior to 1994	17
	Fiscal Adjustment Since 1994	20
	Revenue Developments	21
	Expenditure Developments	22
	Remaining Agenda for Fiscal Consolidation and Reform	23
V	**Monetary Policy and Financial Sector Reforms**	29
	Background	29
	Financial Sector Reforms in 1989–93	29
	Conduct of Monetary Policy Since 1994	32
	Shift to Indirect Instruments of Monetary Management	33
	Interest Rate Deregulation	33
	Foreign Exchange Management	33
	Monetary Developments Since 1991	34
	Commercial Bank Restructuring Efforts	36
	Agenda for Further Reforms	38
VI	**The Social Dimension of Adjustment**	42
	Unemployment	42
	Dynamics of Unemployment	43
	Reasons for Unemployment	43
	Labor Market Reform	44
	Overhauling the Social Safety Net	45
	Subsidy Reform	45

ST. OLAF COLLEGE LIBRARIES

		Page
	Public Works Program	47
	Reform of Unemployment Insurance	47
	Housing Reform: Fostering a Market-Driven Supply Response	48
	Restructuring the Housing Construction Sector	50
	Reforming the Housing Rental Market	51
	Revamping Housing Finance	51
VII	**External Sector Developments**	**53**
	Balance of Payments Developments	53
	Developments Until 1994	53
	Developments Since 1994	54
	Trade Policy	56
	Trade Policy and Reforms Prior to 1994	56
	Trade Reforms Since 1994	58
	Exchange Rate Policy and Exchange Restrictions	58
	Exchange Rate Policy	58
	Reform of the Exchange System	59
	External Debt Burden and Critical Role of External Financing	60
	Future Prospects	61
VIII	**Achievements and Future Challenges**	**63**
	Future Challenges	67

Appendices

I	**Algeria's Hydrocarbon Sector: Evolution and Prospects**	**70**
II	**Dynamics of Unemployment**	**81**

Boxes

IV	1. Tax Reforms	22
	2. Tax Effort in Algeria: Looking at the Denominator	24
	3. Government Wage Expenditure, 1985–96	25
	4. Quasi-Fiscal Deficits: The Algerian Experience	27
V	5. Determinants of Inflation	37
	6. Bank-Enterprises Mechanism	39
	7. Monetary Control and Financial Reforms	40
VI	8. Structure of Unemployment	46
	9. Reform of the Price System and Elimination of Subsidies	48
	10. Housing	49
VII	11. Trade Regime and Foreign Exchange System—Pre-1994 Chronology of Reforms	57
	12. Reschedulings with the Paris and London Clubs	61
VIII	13. Catching Up with Reformers	64
	14. Reducing the Size of the Public Sector in the Economy	65

Tables

II	1. Social Indicators	4
III	2. Chronology of Structural Reforms and Economic Policy Measures	9
	3. Selected Economic and Financial Indicators	12
IV	4. Summary of Central Government Operations	18
	5. Comparative Tax Performance, 1995	28
	6. International Comparison of Petroleum Products' Prices	28
V	7. Monetary Survey	30
	8. Structure of Interest Rates	34

Contents

VII	9. Balance of Payments	55

Appendix Tables

	A1. Exports of Hydrocarbons	74
	A2. Volume of Hydrocarbon Exports	76
	A3. Employment Prospects: High-Growth Scenario	82
	A4. Employment Prospects: Low-Growth Scenario	83

Figures

II	1. Overall Macroeconomic Performance	5
IV	2. Fiscal Indicators	20
	3. Capital Expenditures by Functional Classification	21
	4. Revenue and Overall Balance	23
	5. Current Expenditure by Economic Classification	26
V	6. Interest Rates	35
	7. Monetary Indicators	36
VI	8. Housing Stock and Average Occupancy Ratio	50
	9. Housing Deliveries	51
VII	10. Oil Prices and Real GDP Growth	53
	11. Impact of Oil Price Changes on the Economy	54
	12. Hydrocarbon Export Receipts	54
	13. Trade Flows	56
	14. Debt and Debt Service	56
	15. Exchange Rate Developments	59
VIII	16. Selected Macroeconomic Indicators Compared with Other MENA Countries	66
	17. Selected Socioeconomic Indicators Compared with Other MENA Countries	68

Appendix I

	18. Hydrocarbon Export Receipts	70
	19. Structure of Hydrocarbon Production, Consumption, and Exports, 1993	73

Appendix II

	20. Unemployment Rates Under Low- and High-Growth Scenarios	81

The following symbols have been used throughout this paper:

. . . to indicate that data are not available;

— to indicate that the figure is zero or less than half the final digit shown, or that the item does not exist;

– between years or months (e.g., 1997–98 or January–June) to indicate the years or months covered, including the beginning and ending years or months;

/ between years (e.g., 1997/98) to indicate a crop or fiscal (financial) year.

"Billion" means a thousand million.

Minor discrepancies between constituent figures and totals are due to rounding.

The term "country," as used in this paper, does not in all cases refer to a territorial entity that is a state as understood by international law and practice; the term also covers some territorial entities that are not states, but for which statistical data are maintained and provided internationally on a separate and independent basis.

Preface

This occasional paper offers a review of economic developments in Algeria since the late 1980s, focusing on the period 1994–98, a time of exceptional changes for the Algerian economy that took place against a background of civil strife. Most of this paper draws on the work that was undertaken by the authors during the last four years, underpinning the discussions between the International Monetary Fund and the Algerian authorities while a Stand-By Arrangement, followed by a three-year Extended Arrangement (which expired on May 21, 1998), were in place.

The paper is a collaborative work directed by Karim Nashashibi, who headed the IMF missions to Algeria from mid-1993 to mid-1997. The other principal authors and mission members, who cooperated on the various sections, are Patricia Alonso-Gamo, Stefania Bazzoni, Alain Féler, Nicole Laframboise, and Sebastian Paris Horvitz. The authors would like to acknowledge the contribution of Klaus Enders and Bassirou Sarr, and the comments of Paul Chabrier, Henri Ghesquière, and Ali Hammoudi. The paper also benefited from assistance given by officials of the Bank of Algeria, the Ministry of Finance, and the Ministry of Planning. In particular, we would like to thank Minister of Finance Abdelkrim Harchaoui, Governor Abdelouahab Keramane, Deputy Governor Mohamed Laksaci, Director General of the Treasury Mohamed Younsi, and Kemal Boumerfeg for their valuable comments. The authors would like to thank Geneviève Labeyrie and Moira Sucharov for their invaluable secretarial assistance, as well as Peter Kunzel and Saeed Mahyoub for excellent research assistance. They are also extremely grateful to Martha Bonilla of the External Relations Department for editing the manuscript and coordinating the publication.

The views expressed here are solely those of the authors and do not necessarily reflect the opinions of IMF Executive Directors or the Government of Algeria.

I Overview

This occasional paper assesses Algeria's recent experience with macroeconomic stabilization and systemic transformation from a centrally planned to a market economy. The analysis focuses on the period since 1994 when Algeria embarked on a comprehensive reform program that has benefited from IMF support, first through a one-year Stand-By Arrangement, and, from May 1995, through a three-year arrangement under the Extended Fund Facility. Algeria's efforts have also been supported by several World Bank sectoral lending programs, loans from the Arab Monetary Fund and other donor institutions, extended debt reschedulings from Paris Club official bilateral creditors and commercial banks, and financial assistance from the European Union.

To better understand this experience, this paper provides some background information on Algeria's political history and economic developments during the period preceding the Stand-By Arrangement, and draws some lessons from the reform process.

The paper is organized as follows. Section II describes the geographical, historical, political, and economic setting in which the reforms have been undertaken. Section III provides an overview of the macroeconomic adjustment and structural reform program since 1994. The remaining sections focus on different aspects of the reforms: public finance (Section IV); the conduct of monetary policy and financial sector reforms (Section V); the social aspects of adjustment (Section VI); and external sector developments, including the trade and exchange regime and external debt management (Section VII). Section VIII summarizes Algeria's achievements under the program thus far and highlights challenges that Algeria is likely to face in the coming years in conducting macroeconomic management and making further progress in structural reforms.

II The Setting of Economic Reform

Geographical, Historical, and Political Background

Algeria, with its area of 0.9 million square miles, is the second largest country in Africa. However, 85 percent of its total land mass is occupied by the Saharan desert and is sparsely populated. Most of its current population of about 29.6 million lives along the Mediterranean coast and in the high plains, which are geographically separated from the Saharan desert by mountain chains impeding north-south communication.

Virtually all Algerians are Sunni Muslims, and Islam is the official religion. However, there has always been religious freedom and no restraints are placed on worship for other religions. The population is a mixture of Arab and indigenous Berber, largely integrated. Arabic is the official language, but French is widely used. Most Algerians are bilingual. The Berber language, Tamazight, is also spoken and taught in some schools. Business is mostly conducted in French, though the use of English is increasing. The Berber people, who traditionally live in the mountains of the Rif, Kabyle, and Aurès regions in the northeast Atlas, have a different cultural and linguistic tradition. Except for the desert Tuareg (also known as blue men) who are nomads, they are farmers. Population growth in Algeria, at about 2.2 percent a year, is above average for North Africa. More than 40 percent of the population is younger than 15 years, and about one-half lives in urban areas. Emigration to Europe, once an alternative for Algeria's unemployed, declined from the mid-1970s when France significantly restricted immigration. Life expectancy is 67 years for men and 69 years for women—about average for North Africa. Per capita income in 1996 was about $1,600, compared with $1,200 for Morocco and about $2,000 for Tunisia.

The Algerian desert holds huge hydrocarbon resources, which were first discovered in the 1950s and 1960s. Its proven reserves of crude oil of about 10 billion barrels account for about 1 percent of the world's total reserves. By contrast, those of natural gas, estimated at about 4,000 billion cubic meters, represent close to 5 percent of the world's known reserves. While Algeria has only a small share of world oil production, the hydrocarbon sector represents the central pillar of the Algerian economy. In 1996, it accounted for nearly 30 percent of GDP and contributed to more than 95 percent of merchandise export receipts and more than 60 percent of budgetary revenues. This high hydrocarbon dependence together with the volatility in energy prices has complicated macroeconomic management. Moreover, because of its high capital intensity, the hydrocarbon sector's direct contribution to employment has been small (3 percent).

Most employment opportunities are provided by other sectors, in particular, by manufacturing and construction enterprises (24 percent); the civil service (28 percent); and agriculture (24 percent). The latter, which can make use of only 3 percent of Algeria's land area, produces only one-fourth of the country's food requirements. As a result, Algeria imports large amounts of foodstuff, in particular durum wheat, of which it is the largest importer in the world.

Algeria was originally populated by Berbers and influenced by the Phoenician and Carthaginian civilizations. It was conquered by the Romans[1] in the first century B.C. and Christianized around the second and third centuries. Algeria gradually became Islamized as a result of the Arab conquest during the seventh century, which was followed by several Berber Empires. Early sixteenth century incursions by Spain were resisted by appealing to the Ottomans, who established Algeria as an autonomous region of their Empire until the French conquest, which started in 1830. From the late nineteenth century onward, integration with France increased as a result of a large presence of French settlers. Algerian movements for national independence from France resulted in the uprisings of 1954, the prelude to a war that culminated in the declaration of independence on July 5, 1962.

Algeria thereafter became a socialist, centrally planned economy ruled by a single party, the Front

---

[1]This legacy is reflected in the name of Algerian currency, the dinar, which comes from the *denarius* coin used throughout the Roman Empire.

de libération nationale. Social unrest in 1988 led the Front de libération nationale to adopt a new constitution in 1989 permitting multiparty elections. This allowed the emergence of the Front islamique du salut, which, in 1990, won 54 percent of the vote in the municipal elections and took control of most local governments. By 1991, its popularity had waned somewhat, but the Front islamique du salut still won 47 percent of the vote in the December round of legislative elections and was poised to gain majority control of the parliament before the government canceled the second round in January 1992. This was followed by the replacement of the president, who resigned, by a "five-men presidency," the High State Council. The Front islamique du salut was banned in March 1992 by a Supreme Court decision after terrorist attacks were linked to the party.

Since then, political developments have been dominated by the conflict between the government, the Front islamique du salut, and two more radical groups, the "Armée islamique du salut" and the "Groupe islamique armé." This conflict is estimated to have claimed more than 65,000 lives since 1992.

In 1994, the High State Council was dissolved and Liamine Zéroual was appointed President. In late 1995, capitalizing on the public's general desire to put an end to the violence through political reconciliation, he held presidential elections in which four other candidates participated, including one from the moderate Mouvement pour une société islamique (Hamas). The election registered a high participation rate (75 percent), and President Zéroual won about 60 percent of the vote. In December 1996, a referendum adopted a new constitution that (1) introduced proportional representation in legislative elections; (2) provided the president effectively with a virtual veto power over legislation while imposing a two-term limit; (3) explicitly established Algeria as an Islamic, Arabic, and Tamazigh (Berber) country; and (4) guaranteed the right to form political parties, while making it illegal to base such parties on religion, language, or ethnicity. Within this new constitutional framework, multiparty legislative elections took place in June 1997, and were followed by local and regional elections later in 1997.

The Prereform Economic System

At independence in 1962, Algeria was predominantly an agrarian society with a limited industrial base. During the following 25 years, Algeria pursued a socialist growth model that was inward oriented, emphasizing heavy industrialization and reduced dependency on external investment and imports. The major elements of this model were centralized planning for the economy, the reliance on public enterprises in most services and import-substituting industries, and the creation of large state farms by land nationalization. This strategy was financed by the export receipts of the nationalized hydrocarbon sector. The latter benefited from the oil booms of 1973 and 1979/81 and generated sufficient domestic savings to avoid large accumulation of external debt until the early 1980s.

Within the overall planning framework, each public enterprise had its own annual plan. Purchases of inputs and distribution of output were all approved by the central authorities; wages were fixed according to a national scale, and most prices were controlled. Public enterprise investment was, for the most part, directly financed by the treasury mainly through loans rather than equity participation. This undercapitalization was to pose a major structural problem later on, when those enterprises had to become financially autonomous. Each enterprise was allowed to operate with only one of the five specialized state-owned banks, which provided working capital virtually on demand in the form of overdrafts to fulfill the central plan's objectives.

This strategy originally met with some success. On the one hand, the investment to GDP ratio was maintained at about 45 percent until the late 1970s and the economy grew, on average, by more than 6 percent a year in real terms, compared with 3 percent for middle-income countries as a group. Most social indicators also registered significant improvements. In particular, Algeria's literacy rate rose from 25 percent in the mid-1960s to more than 60 percent in the mid-1980s. Infant mortality rates fell from 150 per thousand to less than 80 over the same period (see Table 1). On the other hand, because of an overvalued exchange rate and negative real interest rates, public enterprises were highly capital intensive, depended on imported inputs, and contributed little to employment creation.

By the early 1980s, the drawbacks of centralized planning were becoming apparent both in public enterprises and state farms, which together accounted for most of Algeria's nonhydrocarbon output. Despite large government investment in state farms, production and yields were not improving significantly, and Algeria's dependence on food imports was increasing rapidly. In addition, the time lags required for completing large public investment projects had become unduly long, notably in the housing sector, which meant that capital was being immobilized for long periods without generating any income. Moreover, most of the new industrial plants were running substantially below capacity. For all of these reasons, the inefficiency of investment rose, as shown by the increase in the incremental capital/output ratio to above 8.

Meanwhile, aggregate demand was fueled by implicit consumption subsidies and high money growth,

II SETTING OF ECONOMIC REFORM

Table 1. Social Indicators

	1989	1990	1991	1992	1993	1994	1995
Population							
Resident population (in millions)	24.4	25.0	25.6	26.3	26.9	27.4	28.0
Rural population (percent of total)	48.5	47.5	46.5	44.4	43.3	45.0	44.2
Population under 15 (percent of total)	39.9	37.9	37.4	38.3	38.3	38.9	38.3
Birth rate (per thousand)	31.0	31.0	30.1	30.4	29.0	...	26.2
Death rate (per thousand)	6.0	6.0	6.0	6.1	6.0	...	5.4
Growth rate (percent)	2.6	2.5	2.5	2.4	2.3	2.1	2.0
Health							
Infant mortality (per thousand)	58.1	...	...	39.0	...	...	33.5
Population per physician (in thousands)	1.1	1.0	1.0	1.0	1.0	...	...
Education							
Primary enrollment (net)[1]	94.0	93.0	...	94.0	95.0	95.0	...
Secondary enrollment (net)[1]	61.0	54.0	...	55.0	55.0	55.0	...
Illiteracy rate[2]	...	42.6	...	...	...	...	38.4
Employment							
Labor force (percent of total population)	22.2	23.4	23.8	24.1	24.4	24.8	27.0
Unemployment (percent of labor force)[3]	18.1	20.3	21.3	23.2	24.4	24.8	28.0
Income							
GDP per capita in U.S. dollars[4]	2,869.4	3,523.9	2,046.8	1,822.8	1,852.6	1,529.5	1,477.1

Sources: Algerian authorities; *Statistical Yearbook of Algeria 1991*; United Nations Educational, Scientific and Cultural Organization, *Statistical Yearbook 1996*; World Bank, *World Development Report 1995*, and *Social Indicators of Development 1996*.
[1] Percentage of age group over same age group enrolled in education.
[2] In percent of population at least 15 years old.
[3] For 1995, new survey data are provided.
[4] Converted at the official exchange rate.

which reflected mainly the financing of public enterprises by commercial banks together with the monetization of large fiscal deficits. As demand continued to outstrip supply, rationing became prevalent. Many consumer goods were increasingly scarce or unavailable on the official market despite Algeria's large hydrocarbon export receipts. The combination of excess liquidity with commodity shortages and the administrative allocation of foreign exchange was reflected in an increasing discrepancy between the parallel and the official exchange rates. The price of the U.S. dollar on the parallel foreign exchange market rose from two times the official rate in the early 1980s to five times in 1985.

Reverse Oil Shock of 1986 and First Attempts at Reform

The rigidities and weaknesses of the centrally planned system became much more apparent when the reverse oil shock of 1986 caused both Algeria's terms of trade and hydrocarbon budgetary revenues to drop by about 50 percent. In response to the crisis, the authorities did not adjust the exchange rate, but initiated several measures of macroeconomic stabilization and structural reforms. At first, the pace of adjustment was sluggish and macroeconomic imbalances worsened. The overall budget deficit reached a record 13.7 percent of GDP in 1988 as cuts in government expenditure failed to compensate for the revenue decline (Figure 1). In the absence of a financial market, fiscal deficits were monetized or financed through the buildup of external debt. The ratio of external debt to GDP rose from 30 percent in 1985 to 41 percent in 1988, while the debt service to exports ratio jumped from 35 percent to 78 percent reflecting the shortening of maturities. In the presence of extensive price controls, monetization did not result in a large increase in inflation, but rather in greater rationing in the goods markets, a further buildup of excess liquidity, and higher prices in the thriving informal economy. The ratio of broad money to GDP, which stood at 76 percent in 1985, increased further to 79 percent in 1988. In addition, negative real interest rates and an overvalued currency reinforced the bias toward capital-intensive techniques and imports.

Macroeconomic adjustment efforts were strengthened over 1989–91, when the authorities embarked

Figure 1. Overall Macroeconomic Performance

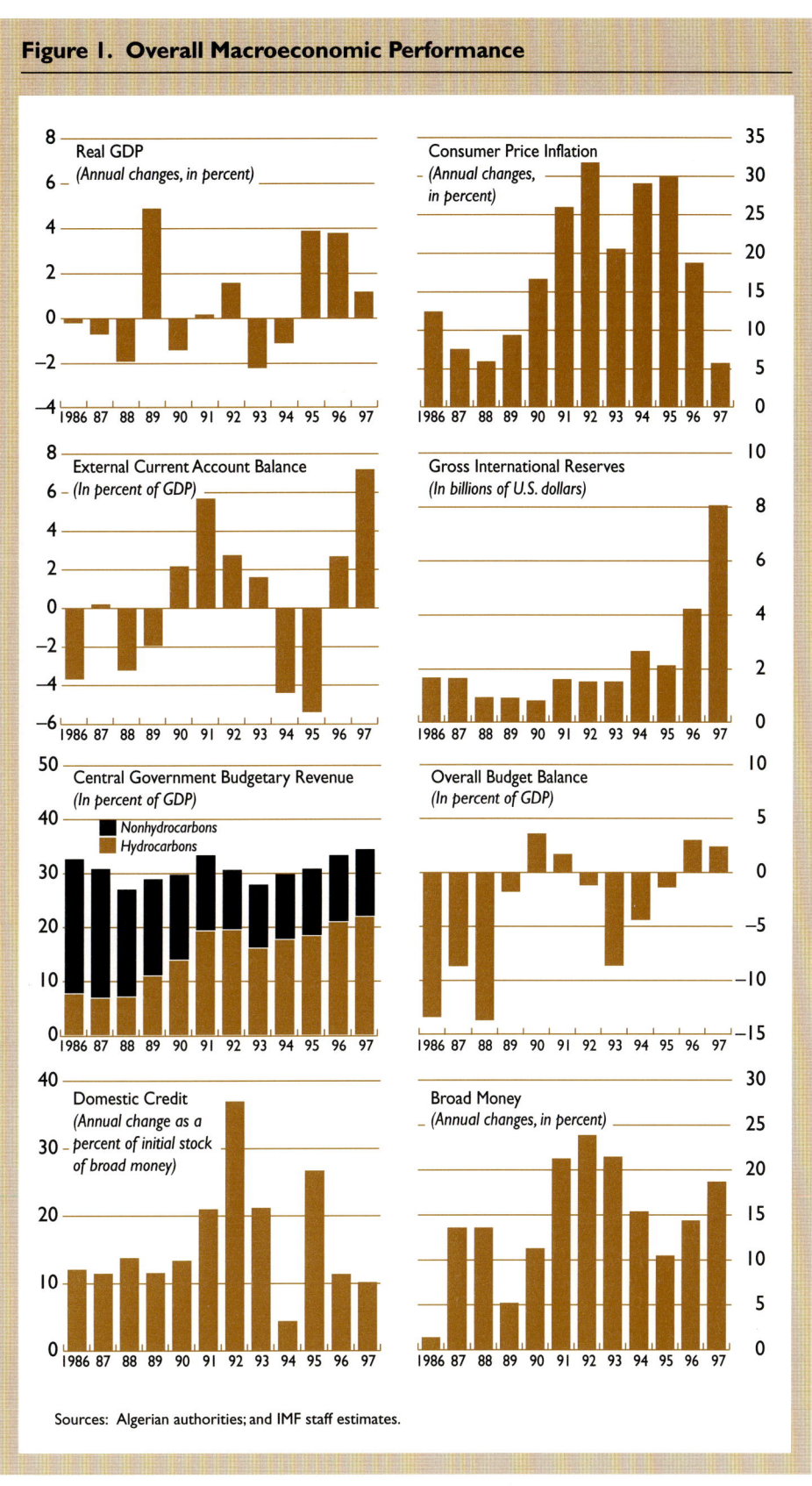

Sources: Algerian authorities; and IMF staff estimates.

II SETTING OF ECONOMIC REFORM

on two IMF-supported programs (1989 and 1991) that entailed strict demand management policies and substantial exchange rate depreciation. Government expenditure restraint, together with higher hydrocarbon revenues on account of both favorable oil prices and exchange rate depreciation, resulted in the emergence of fiscal surpluses. Tight fiscal policy provided the underpinning for a marked slowdown in money growth, permitting excess liquidity to be partially absorbed.

Tighter demand policies coupled with substantial trade liberalization measures and adjustments in the nominal exchange rate resulted in a real effective depreciation of more than 60 percent between 1988 and 1991. Together with the absorption of excess liquidity, the depreciation reduced excess demand for foreign exchange, and the discount of the Algerian dinar in the parallel market was cut from a factor of five in 1988 to a factor of less than two in 1991. However, as a result of the depreciation and of the partial liberalization of domestic prices and interest rates, inflation, as measured by the consumer price index (CPI), increased to 22.8 percent in 1991 compared with 10.3 percent on average over the five preceding years.

On the external side, the combination of expenditure switching and reducing policies, together with favorable oil prices, contributed to a shift of the current account balance from a deficit of 3 percent of GDP in 1988 to a surplus of 6 percent of GDP in 1991. Developments in the capital account were less favorable as Algeria's capacity to contract new external borrowing reached its limits, while amortization payments rose substantially in part because of the increasing reliance on suppliers' credits of less than a three-year maturity. As a result, the debt-service ratio in 1991 was still at about its 1988 level, notwithstanding much higher oil exports proceeds in dollar terms.

The 1991 IMF-supported adjustment program could not be fully implemented owing to three main factors. First, the decision by the authorities not to resort to a comprehensive external debt rescheduling with the Paris and the London Clubs severely constrained the amount of exceptional financing available for the program. Second, part of the external financing programmed for 1991 failed to materialize, which contributed to a contraction of imports of more than 20 percent in dollar terms and a fall in output, particularly in the manufacturing and construction sectors. Third, the program was not grounded on a broad consensus among social partners. Employers felt that the exchange rate adjustment had been adverse to their operations, since it had increased the cost of imported inputs and external debt service, whereas this increase could not be passed on to domestic prices, which had been liberalized only partially. As for labor unions, they were not made a party to the agreement and were unwilling to accept the decline in real wages brought about by the devaluation of the Algerian dinar, particularly in the absence of an adequate social safety net. This forced the government to agree, just before the first round of parliamentary elections at the end of 1991, to large wage increases to be granted during 1992.

On the structural front, important reforms were introduced in the late 1980s and early 1990s to gradually decentralize the decision-making process and develop market mechanisms. The first measures took place in agriculture with the breakup in 1987 of about 3,500 large state farms into smaller private cooperatives and individual farms holding long-term usufruct rights. These reforms resulted in sharp productivity increases, turning agriculture into the engine of growth for the Algerian economy (excluding hydrocarbons). In the industrial and construction sectors, nearly all national public enterprises were granted legal and operational autonomy in 1988. This was followed by the adoption in 1990 of a program to write off a large amount of the nonperforming foreign and domestic debt of public enterprises, which had accumulated over years of direct state controls, and to recapitalize the commercial banks. The program was financed by a special restructuring fund supported by budgetary allocations and by the World Bank Enterprise and Financial Sector Adjustment Loan. Concurrently, a new legal and regulatory framework for the financial sector was established by the 1990 money and credit law. This new law devolved to the Bank of Algeria the responsibility for monetary policy and oversight of the banking system, and eliminated direct financing by the treasury of new public enterprise investment. In addition, to promote competition, the authorities authorized the creation of private banks and abolished the practice of assigning each public enterprise to a particular commercial bank. Finally, structural reforms in the labor market introduced greater flexibility in wage setting and labor contracts and authorized labor shedding for economic reasons combined with provision of severance payments.

The potential benefits of this liberalization and reform process were stymied, however, by the lack of integration of the various measures into a comprehensive framework, and the absence of some key steps indispensable for creating an efficient market economy. For instance, agricultural reform did not include the attribution of property rights, thus hindering the ability of private farmers to access commercial credit. As for public enterprises, their financial situation continued to be constrained by ongoing price controls by the Ministry of Supply and by high severance costs for labor shedding. This led to the accumulation of further losses, which could be financed by loans from commercial banks whose recapitalization was not accompanied by sufficient prudential regulations.

As a result of their piecemeal nature, Algeria's first attempts at structural adjustment following the reverse oil shock failed to improve significantly the efficiency of resource allocation and to put the economy on a sustainable growth path. Real nonhydrocarbon GDP declined on average by 1.5 percent a year during 1986–91. This dismal outcome reflected a stagnation in manufacturing and falling output in the construction and services sectors that more than outweighed a persistently strong growth performance in agriculture.

Policy Reversal of 1992–93

Starting in 1992, against the backdrop of political uncertainties, civil strife, and dwindling access to external financing, the pace of structural reforms slowed down and macroeconomic imbalances widened. The authorities' strategy in 1992–93 aimed at fully meeting external debt service, which had reached 80 percent of export proceeds, while supporting economic activity with an expansionary fiscal policy. In particular, government consumption increased by 2 percentage points of GDP over the period, while the ratio of government investment to GDP increased from 6 percent in 1991 to 8.4 percent in 1993. As a result, the government's savings-investment balance deteriorated by more than 10 percentage points of GDP. These large fiscal imbalances (8.7 percent of GDP budget deficit in 1993) also reflected the lack of exchange rate adjustment—which undermined hydrocarbon and trade-related budget revenues—and widespread government subsidies on basic consumption items, which accounted for 5 percent of GDP annually during 1992–93.

The authorities' relaxation of fiscal discipline adversely affected monetary developments through the monetization of budget deficits. Rapid monetary expansion generated inflationary pressures, which contributed to the increasing overvaluation of the Algerian dinar. Such pressures were partially repressed, particularly in 1993, when administered controls on prices and trade were tightened, and a significant drop in the income velocity of broad money signaled the reemergence of a monetary overhang.

The inconsistency between expansionary demand management policies and the reluctance to adjust the exchange rate, coupled with an external debt strategy that sought to avoid a formal debt rescheduling and declining oil prices, resulted in a deterioration in the external current account. The authorities' response was to reintroduce trade and payments restrictions and tighten administrative controls. These measures exacerbated resource misallocation and caused a drop in capacity utilization, a drop in investment in the nonhydrocarbon sector, widespread shortages of various consumer items, and an increase in unemployment from 20 percent of the labor force in 1990 to 24 percent in 1993.

III Macroeconomic Stabilization and Structural Reforms Since 1994

The severe imbalances inherited from previous years deteriorated further at the beginning of 1994, when a further fall in oil prices, coupled with growing civil strife and the drying-up of external financing brought the economy to the brink of balance of payment crisis. This deterioration compelled the authorities to formulate a comprehensive structural adjustment program that received the support of the IMF in May 1994, with a one-year Stand-By Arrangement and, from May 1995, with a three-year arrangement under the Extended Fund Facility. This section summarizes the main objectives and reform strategy pursued under this program as well as Algeria's macroeconomic performance during 1994–97. Sections IV to VII examine in greater detail economic developments in each major policy reform area.

Objectives and Economic Policy Strategy

The adjustment program in place since early 1994 was structured around four major objectives: (1) to promote a high rate of economic growth so as to absorb the increase in the labor force and gradually reduce unemployment; (2) to ensure a rapid convergence of inflation toward rates prevailing in industrial countries; (3) to mitigate the transitional costs of structural adjustment on the most vulnerable segments of the population; and (4) to restore balance of payments viability while ensuring adequate levels of foreign exchange reserves.

In pursuit of these objectives, Algeria decided to ease the immediate constraint arising from its high external debt service with a comprehensive debt rescheduling amounting to more than $17 billion over the four program years. This was to be complemented by an additional amount of $5.5 billion in exceptional balance of payments support from the IMF, other international and regional institutions, and bilateral donors. The availability of such a large amount of external financing allowed an increase in absorption during the first program year as reflected by a shift in the external current account balance from a surplus of 1.9 percent of GDP in 1993 to a deficit of 4.3 percent of GDP in 1994. In this regard, Algeria's experience is somewhat different from the typical adjustment process that entails an initial contraction of aggregate demand.

The temporary relaxation of the external constraint was also to provide enough breathing space for the timely implementation of a three-pronged medium-term structural reform strategy, which consisted of the following (Table 2).

- the realignment of relative prices and the abolition of external trade and payment restrictions to alleviate the shortages in a number of basic goods and achieve efficient resource allocation;
- public expenditure restraint and a tight monetary policy designed to contain aggregate demand and bring about, over time, internal and external balance; and
- the establishment of the institutional and market mechanisms necessary to complete the transition from a centrally planned to a diversified market economy (Table 3).

Realignment of Relative Prices and External Trade Liberalization

The realignment of relative prices was pursued with an active exchange rate policy and further liberalization of domestic prices. At the onset of the program, a 50 percent exchange rate devaluation corrected for the overvaluation of the Algerian dinar that had developed in 1992 and 1993, when the nominal exchange rate had remained broadly stable despite growing inflationary pressures. This was followed by a gradual shift in the exchange rate regime from a peg to a basket of major currencies to a managed float, which allowed for greater flexibility in the event of adverse terms of trade shocks. In addition, to increase the role of market forces in the determination of the exchange rate, an interbank foreign exchange market was introduced at the end of 1995. Overall, between 1993 and 1996, the real effective exchange rate depreciated by about 30 percent as a

Table 2. Chronology of Structural Reforms and Economic Policy Measures

Structural Reforms and Policy Measures	Date
Exchange regime	
• Adjustments in the Algerian dinar exchange rate between April and September 1994 that cumulatively amounted to a depreciation of 50 percent in terms of U.S. dollars.	1994
• Introduction of a managed float through fixing sessions between the Bank of Algeria and commercial banks.	1994
• Transformation of fixing sessions into an interbank foreign exchange market with banks and other authorized intermediaries.	1995
• Establishment of *bureaux de change*.	1996
• Implementation of an exchange rate policy that aims to ensure external competitiveness, supported by appropriate financial policies.	1994–96
Trade and payments liberalization	
• Introduction of a negative list of imports and liberalization of 10 basic staples whose imports had been subject to technical and professional criteria.	1994
• Unification at 50 percent of surrender requirements for export proceeds with the exception of hydrocarbon products.	1994
• Elimination of all export prohibitions, except for items of historical and archeological significance.	1994
• Liberalization of imports of used professional and industrial equipment.	1994
• Elimination of the negative list of imports introduced in April 1994.	1994
• Elimination of minimum maturity requirement on external borrowing for imports of capital goods.	1995
• Elimination of the requirement for importers of certain goods to observe professional and technical criteria (medicines, milk, semolina, flour, and wheat).	1995
• Authorization of payments for health and education abroad:	
—By the Bank of Algeria subject to annual ceilings.	1995
—By commercial banks subject to specific ceilings, and by the Bank of Algeria above these ceilings.	1996
• Reduction of the maximum tariff duty rate:	
—From 60 percent to 50 percent.	1996
—From 50 percent to 45 percent.	1997
• Authorization of payments for other nontourism expenditures abroad (e.g., business travel, salary transfers, advertising expenses) by commercial banks up to specific ceilings, and by the Bank of Algeria above these ceilings.	1996
• Convertibility of the Algerian dinar for current account transactions. Algeria accepted the obligations of the IMF, Article VIII.	1997
Price liberalization	
• Transfer of several products from the administered price category to the controlled profit margin category.	1994
• Elimination of controlled profit margins for all but five sensitive products (sugar, cereals, edible oils, school supplies, and medicines).	1994
• Freeing of agricultural input prices.	1994
• Introduction of a mechanism ensuring:	
—Six-monthly revisions of the sale price of crude oil from Sonatrach to the refineries.	1994
—Quarterly revisions of the price of electricity and gas according to inflation trends.	1994
• Freeing of construction prices for social housing.	1994
• Limiting support prices for agriculture to potato seed and wheat.	1994
• Elimination of generalized consumption subsidies:	
—Petroleum products.	1995
—Food products.	1994–96
• Elimination of controls on profit margins and deregulation of prices for sugar, nonwheat cereals, edible oil, and school supplies.	1995
• Increasing rents in public housing by 30 percent.	1995–97
Public enterprise reform and private sector development	
• Introduction of new Investment Code that allows foreign participation in domestic banks.	1994
• Extending the legal framework for public enterprise privatization:	
—Authorizing the sale of units of public enterprises and private equity participation in most public enterprises up to 49 percent.	1994
—Authorizing 100 percent private equity participation in most public enterprises.	1995
• Liquidation of 827 of 1,300 local public enterprises.	1994–97
• Granting of autonomy to 22 large public enterprises whose large losses had required special monitoring and restructuring programs.	1994–96
• Adoption of a first privatization program in collaboration with the World Bank targeting about 200 small local enterprises.	1996
• Adoption of restructuring plans for 10 public-importing and distribution agencies, the railroads, and the gas and electricity company.	1996
• Publication of a program for the privatization of 250 large public enterprises over 1998–99.	1997

III MACROECONOMIC STABILIZATION AND STRUCTURAL REFORMS

Table 2 *(continued)*

Structural Reforms and Policy Measures	Date
Monetary policy and financial sector reform	
• Elimination of ceilings on bank lending rates while imposing a limit of 5 percentage points on banks' spreads.	1994
• Introduction of minimum reserve requirements of 3 percent on bank deposits renumerated at 11 percent a year.	1994
• Audit of the state-owned commercial banks in collaboration with the World Bank.	1994–96
• Financial restructuring and recapitalization of public commercial banks, through both cash injections and debt conversion operations.	1994–96
• Development of the money market:	
—Introduction of an auction system for central bank credit.	1995
—Introduction of an auction system for treasury bills.	1995
—Introduction of open-market operations.	1996
• Imposing a capital adequacy ratio of 4 percent, to be increased to the Bank of International Settlements standard of 8 percent by 1999.	1995
• Strengthening prudential regulations that limit risk concentrations and establish clear rules for loan classification and provisioning.	1995
• Elimination of the 5 percentage point limit on banks' interest rate spreads.	1996
• Decision to transform the Caisse nationale d'épargne et de prévoyance into a mortgage commercial bank in early 1997.	
• Making preparations for the introduction of a capital market:	1996–98
—Creation of the Commission for Stock Market Organization and Supervision.	
—Creation of the Securities Exchange Management Company.	
—First issue of bonds by Sonatrach (DA 12 billion) in February 1998.	
• Integration of the Caisse nationale d'épargne et de prévoyance into the banking system, in conjunction with:	1997
—Establishment of a housing finance system.	
—Implementation of an audit-based plan for institutional strengthening.	
—Definition and application of a ratio for converting deposits on house-savings accounts into housing loans.	
• Introduction of a deposit insurance scheme.	1997
• Preparation with the World Bank of a modernization program of the payment system.	1998
Public finance	
• Broadening the coverage of the VAT by reducing exemptions.	1994–96
• Increasing the duties on luxury products and consumer appliances.	1994
• Increasing the tax rate on reinvested profits from 5 percent to 33 percent, as a step toward the unification of the dual corporate tax rate.	1994
• Eliminating the tax exemption for interest earnings from treasury bonds.	1994
• Eliminating the top VAT rate of 40 percent, while increasing the share of the VAT receipts accruing to the central government.	1995
• Introduction of an individual tax identification number to each taxpayer.	1996
• Extension of the VAT to petroleum products.	1997
• Expenditure priorities reordered, including elimination of consumer subsidies and a tight incomes policy.	1994–96
• Decision to budgetize the financing of all new projects of public housing for rent.	1996
• Public expenditure review in collaboration with the World Bank.	1996
Social safety net and social issues	
• Elimination of the cash allowance for nonincome earning households; other allowances incorporated into wages and social benefits, with financial responsibility for family allowances transferred to the government.	1994
• Introduction of an unemployment insurance scheme.	1994
• Introduction of a public work scheme.	1994
Labor market	
• Study of the labor market, in collaboration with the World Bank, aimed at improving mobility and flexibility while protecting workers' rights.	1997–98
Agricultural sector	
• Limit agricultural price supports to wheat.	1996
• Cereals: Establish a system of reference prices linked to world market prices, with the aim of enhancing the effectiveness of the system and gradually reducing the fiscal burden.	1995
• Reform land tenure with a view to increasing marketability and collateralization of land holdings.	1995
• Preparation of draft regulations on enhancing marketability and values in the land tenure system.	1995
• Draft law establishing the procedures for the privatization of agricultural land submitted to the National Assembly.	1997
Housing sector	
• Identification, in collaboration with the World Bank, of measures aimed at encouraging private investment in the housing sector.	1995–98
• Organization of a mortgage market.	1995–98

Realignment of Relative Prices and External Trade Liberalization

Table 2 (concluded)

Structural Reforms and Policy Measures	Date
• Review rents for social housing and introduce regulations establishing a system of periodic adjustments based on changes in operating costs.	1995
• The Caisse nationale d'épargne et de prévoyance becomes the Housing Bank (Banque de l'habitat).	1997
• Creation of the Mortgage Refinance Company (Société de refinancement hypothécaire).	1997
• Creation of the Mortgage Loan Guarantee Company (Société de garantie du crédit immobilier).	1997
• Creation of the real estate guarantee fund (fonds de garantie et de caution mutuelle de la promotion immobilière).	1997
Environmental policy	
• Formulation, in collaboration with the World Bank, of measures aimed at establishing a comprehensive strategy for protecting the environment.	1995–98
Data enhancements	
• Improvements in the balance of payments compilation system, inter alia by:	
—Adopting a stricter residency criterion that conforms more closely with the recommendations of the *Balance of Payments Manual* and those used in monetary statistics.	1995–98
—Compiling data quarterly, and publishing them in a new periodical bulletin of the Bank of Algeria.	1996–97

result of nominal depreciation combined with tight demand management and incomes policies. This gain in external competitiveness should help foster greater diversification of the economy toward nonhydrocarbon tradable activities.

As for domestic relative prices, the adjustment process entailed the liberalization of administered prices and interest rates and the replacement of a generalized and inefficient system of subsidies by targeted transfers. Notwithstanding a partial liberalization in the early 1990s, interest rates were still negative in real terms at the beginning of 1994, thereby distorting relative factor prices and resource allocation. The first measure toward market-determined interest rates consisted in abolishing, in 1994, the ceiling on commercial banks' lending rates to the public. However, this was combined with the introduction of a temporary cap on banks' interest rate spreads—to prevent excessive lending rates in the event of collusion among banks—which was eliminated in December 1995. The deregulation of interest rates, together with the deceleration in inflation brought about by tight demand management policies, led to the emergence of positive real interest rates in 1996.

At the beginning of 1994, Algeria had a generalized system of subsidies that cost the budget more than 5 percent of GDP and had led to speculative inventory accumulation, shortages, and parallel markets. In addition, large quantities of subsidized goods were smuggled to neighboring countries. The elimination of these subsidies required a major liberalization of the price system as well as substantial increases in administered prices. In 1994, prices of all inputs for agriculture and housing construction were freed, and controls on retail prices and profit margins were lifted for most goods and services except for a limited number of products including a few essential food staples, energy products, and public transportation fares that remained subsidized. The generalized subsidies on these goods were eliminated over the following two years as prices were raised toward their opportunity cost. This was done progressively so as to mitigate the social impact and repercussions on the general price level. Over 1994–96, prices of subsidized food and petroleum products had to be increased on average by almost 200 percent to reach international prices. For petroleum products, the implicit subsidy was eliminated, as the transfer price from the national oil company to the refineries was set at the world price level, with adjustments every six months in line with international oil prices and exchange rate developments. The small remaining subsidy on gas and electricity consumer tariffs (less than 1 percent of GDP in 1996) was completely eliminated in 1997.

To cushion the impact of the exchange rate depreciation and the elimination of generalized subsidies on the most vulnerable social groups, the authorities embarked in 1994 on a reform of the social safety net. The previous system, introduced in 1992, consisted of cash transfers that were both poorly targeted and costly to the budget. It was replaced by a decentralized public works program compensating those able to work for their participation in a public activity on a full-time basis. This compensation was

III MACROECONOMIC STABILIZATION AND STRUCTURAL REFORMS

Table 3. Selected Economic and Financial Indicators

	1986	1987	1988	1989	1990	1991	1992	1993	1994	1995	1996	1997
						(Percent change)						
National income and prices												
GDP at constant prices	-0.2	-0.7	-1.9	4.9	-1.4	0.2	1.6	-2.2	-0.9	3.9	3.8	1.2
Hydrocarbon sector	1.2	7.1	-1.9	8.0	4.3	1.4	1.1	-0.8	-2.5	4.4	6.3	6.0
Other sectors[1]	-0.6	-2.2	-1.9	4.5	-3.9	-1.2	1.8	-2.6	-0.3	3.7	3.3	-0.7
GDP deflator	2.5	8.8	9.4	15.1	27.3	48.0	20.0	22.0	27.7	28.4	22.2	8.0
Consumer price index (average)	12.4	7.5	5.9	9.3	16.6	25.9	31.7	20.5	29.0	29.8	18.6	5.7
External sector[2]												
Exports, f.o.b.	-38.1	12.0	-15.8	21.4	36.4	-2.8	-8.7	-9.5	-14.6	15.3	28.7	4.6
Of which: hydrocarbons	-39.0	12.7	-16.6	21.5	34.8	-3.1	-8.3	-10.0	-12.9	13.0	29.9	4.3
Imports, f.o.b.	-9.2	-14.1	5.3	23.2	3.2	-20.5	6.4	-3.7	14.5	10.4	-10.0	-11.0
Terms of trade	-43.6	14.1	-23.0	10.6	23.6	-10.4	-13.3	-8.7	-8.7	-3.0	16.0	3.7
Real effective exchange rate[3]	9.3	-15.7	-17.8	-13.0	-22.1	-39.5	2.7	20.3	-14.1	-16.2	2.5	9.6
Money and credit												
Net foreign assets of the banking system[4]	-2.5	-0.1	0.1	-1.0	0.0	5.2	-0.4	-0.6	6.5	-4.7	13.5	23.7
Domestic credit[4]	12.0	11.4	13.8	11.5	13.3	20.9	33.5	23.7	4.3	26.6	11.3	13.4
Credit to the government (net)[5]	10.9	9.7	9.3	10.7	-3.8	-2.1	0.0	17.8	-9.4	-9.3	-15.1	-4.5
Credit to the economy[5]	1.0	1.6	4.4	0.8	17.1	23.0	33.5	5.9	13.8	35.9	26.4	17.9
Money and quasi-money	1.4	13.6	13.6	5.2	11.3	21.3	23.9	21.5	15.4	10.5	14.4	18.5
Liquidity ratio (in percent of GDP)[6]	78.9	79.3	78.7	70.9	58.5	42.9	44.6	49.2	45.8	38.7	34.8	36.7
						(In percent of GDP)						
Overall budget balance (deficit -)	-13.4	-8.7	-13.7	-1.8	3.6	1.7	-1.2	-8.7	-4.4	-1.4	3.0	2.4
Revenue	32.3	30.5	26.7	28.6	28.8	32.3	30.3	27.6	29.5	30.4	33.1	34.1
Hydrocarbons[7]	7.5	6.7	6.9	10.8	13.7	19.1	19.3	15.9	17.5	18.2	20.8	21.8
Nonhydrocarbons[8]	24.8	23.8	19.8	17.8	15.1	13.1	11.1	11.6	12.0	12.3	12.2	12.3
Expenditure[9]	45.7	39.2	40.4	30.4	25.2	30.6	31.5	36.2	33.9	32.0	30.1	31.7
Current expenditure	23.2	21.9	22.3	19.7	17.4	22.2	22.6	24.9	23.4	22.5	22.0	23.7
Investment	14.6	12.5	12.4	10.1	8.2	6.2	6.9	8.7	8.0	7.3	7.0	7.4
Other[9]	7.9	4.8	5.7	0.6	-0.4	2.2	2.0	2.6	2.6	2.0	1.0	0.6
Domestic bank financing	8.5	5.1	6.8	1.4	3.1	-1.8	1.1	6.3	-6.7	-5.4	-5.6	-3.7
External current account (deficit -)	-3.6	0.9	-2.6	-2.2	2.5	5.7	2.8	1.6	-4.4	-5.4	2.7	7.3
External debt	34.7	39.1	41.7	47.0	43.0	60.6	52.0	53.0	70.3	78.6	73.4	68.7
						(In billions of U.S. dollars)						
Exports, f.o.b.	8.1	9.0	7.6	9.6	12.9	12.4	11.5	10.4	8.9	10.3	13.2	13.8
Imports, f.o.b.	8.5	7.3	7.7	9.5	9.8	7.8	8.3	8.0	9.2	10.1	9.1	8.1
Interest payments	1.6	1.6	2.1	2.0	2.2	2.3	2.3	1.9	1.8	2.3	2.2	2.1

Realignment of Relative Prices and External Trade Liberalization

Current account (deficit –)	-2.2	0.2	-2.0	-0.9	1.4	2.4	1.3	0.8	-1.8	-2.2	1.2	3.5
Overall balance (deficit –)	-1.5	-0.3	-0.8	-0.6	-0.2	0.5	0.2	0.0	-4.4	-6.3	-2.1	1.2
Gross official reserves (end of period)	1.7	1.7	0.9	0.9	0.8	1.6	1.5	1.5	2.6	2.1	4.2	8.0
External debt	21.1	24.6	24.7	26.1	26.7	27.0	26.1	26.4	29.5	32.5	33.5	30.0
(In billions of Algerian dinars, unless otherwise indicated)												
GDP (current prices)	286	306	350	423	556	844	1,045	1,162	1,471	1,966	2,495	2,716
Crude oil export unit value (in U.S. dollars/barrel)	14.8	18.5	18.5	16.2	24.4	20.4	20.1	17.8	16.3	17.6	21.7	19.8
Exchange rate (Algerian dinar/U.S. dollar) (end of period)	4.8	4.9	6.7	8.0	12.2	21.4	22.8	24.1	42.9	52.2	56.2	58.0

Sources: Algerian authorities; and IMF staff estimates and projections.

[1]GDP at market prices.
[2]In U.S. dollars terms.
[3]Twelve-month changes in the total trade-weighted IMF Information Notice System index. A decrease in the index implies a depreciation.
[4]Annual change as a percentage of broad money at the beginning of the period.
[5]The percent changes for the 12-month periods ending December 1993 and December 1997 exclude the impact of two financial restructuring packages involving the swap of government bonds for public enterprises' commercial debt. The amounts involved are respectively DA 275.5 billion in 1993 (or 53.4 percent of end-December 1992 money stock) and DA 186.7 billion in the first quarter of 1997 (or 20.3 percent of end-December 1996 money stock).
[6]Ratio of the average broad money (M2) stock during the year to GDP.
[7]Including dividends on current profits paid by Sonatrach.
[8]Including grants.
[9]Including special accounts, net lending, and allocation to the Rehabilitation Fund.

set at a level lower than the minimum wage to target the truly unemployed whose opportunity cost was below the compensation received. The new social safety net system also provided an increase in the transfers received by pensioners and disabled who are unable to work (see Section VI).

To provide appropriate market incentives to the productive sector, the realignment in relative prices was accompanied by a major liberalization of the external trade and payments system (see Section VII). In 1994, the authorities dismantled the cumbersome system of controls that had been introduced during the policy reversal of 1992–93. In particular, they abolished the administrative foreign exchange allocation that was established in 1992 for authorized imports. This gave importers free access to foreign exchange for all but a short list of imports that were temporarily prohibited. The negative list was eliminated at the end of 1994, and today, Algeria's trade system remains free of quantitative restrictions. To support the trade liberalization program, the authorities lowered the maximum custom duty rate from 60 percent in 1994 to 45 percent as of January 1, 1997, and reduced the number of tariff rates. Significant progress was also achieved toward the current account convertibility of the Algerian dinar with the liberalization of all invisible payments. Tourism expenses were liberalized by the end of 1997, achieving current account convertibility.

Macroeconomic Policies and Performance

To achieve the macroeconomic objectives of the program, the government relied primarily on strong fiscal adjustment supported by a strict incomes policy and an active exchange rate policy. This was complemented by a tight monetary policy and the emergence of positive real interest rates.

The central government overall fiscal balance shifted from a deficit close to 9 percent of GDP in 1993 to a surplus of more than 3 percent of GDP in 1996 and 2.4 percent in 1997.[2] This achievement, which contributed markedly to reducing the economy's saving-investment gap, was made possible by a broad consensus among the government, labor, public enterprises, and the private sector. The strong fiscal performance reflected both government revenue increases, which benefited greatly from the depreciation of the Algerian dinar and, in 1996, from favorable world oil prices. Firm public expenditure restraint—especially with respect to wages, subsidies, and investment also contributed to this outcome. The emergence of a fiscal surplus was intended to decrease the budget's vulnerability to potential oil price declines and to provide flexibility in addressing potential claims on public resources during the rest of the transition period, as well as making more resources available for the development of the private sector.

Fiscal retrenchment provided the underpinning for a tight monetary policy that resulted in a fall of the liquidity ratio from 49 percent in 1993 to 36 percent in 1996, thereby eliminating the liquidity overhang that had accumulated during 1992–93. Ceilings on money markets and commercial banks' lending rates were abolished in the context of a shift toward the use of indirect instruments of liquidity control. To this end, the Bank of Algeria imposed a reserve requirement on commercial banks in 1994 and, subsequently, introduced a repurchase auction system for bank refinancing as well as open market operations.

The program that Algeria implemented from 1994 achieved impressive results in stabilizing the macroeconomic situation. Inflation, which reached 39 percent in 1994, mostly on account of the impact of the large initial depreciation of the Algerian dinar and adjustments of administered prices of subsidized commodities, decelerated to 6 percent at the end of 1997. The tightening of demand management policies coupled with the depreciation of the Algerian dinar and the availability of a large amount of exceptional financing also resulted in a significant strengthening of Algeria's external position, with gross official foreign exchange reserves increasing from $1.5 billion at the end of 1993 (1.8 months of imports) to $2.1 billion at the end of 1995 (2.1 months of imports), and further to $8.0 billion at the end of 1997 (8 months of imports), partly owing to favorable oil prices. Moreover, the 2 percent decline in real GDP in 1993 was reduced to 1 percent in 1994 before giving way to real growth rates of about 4 percent in 1995 and 1996. This improved growth performance, which was driven by a strong export-led expansion in the hydrocarbon sector, a rebound of agriculture after two consecutive drought years, and an expansion in the construction and service sectors, led to an increase in per capita income in both 1995 and 1996 after a five-year decline. The increase was reinforced in 1996 by an improvement of more than 16 percent in Algeria's terms of trade. Nevertheless, manufacturing output continued to decline, partly because of import liberalization that exposed Algerian products to foreign competition, and partly because of the impact of macroeconomic policies that reduced domestic demand. Structural problems related to the obsolescence of capital equipment and product lines in

---

[2]The 1996 budget surplus also reflected the impact of particularly favorable oil prices. Without this impact, the surplus would have been 0.7 percentage points of GDP.

many public enterprises, as well as poor management, foreshadowed a difficult and long process of modernization and restructuring for Algerian manufacturing enterprises. Growth was still positive in 1997, but yet again adversely affected by a drought.

Structural and Institutional Reforms

Until the beginning of 1994, resource allocation in Algeria had been governed mostly by administrative decisions and direct state controls on prices, production, and credit. Beyond the realignment of prices and the liberalization of the external trade and payment systems, Algeria introduced measures aimed at changing the role of the state from the producer of most goods and services to the provider of administrative services, education, health, and a regulatory framework that is essential for the proper functioning of an efficient market economy. In particular, headway was made in restructuring public enterprises to facilitate their privatization, in strengthening property rights to promote private sector development, and in restructuring the financial sector to ensure more efficient credit allocation.

Efforts had been made prior to 1994 toward the restructuring of public enterprises. In particular, most public enterprises were granted legal and financial autonomy while being financially rehabilitated through debt forgiveness by the treasury and the swap of government bonds for nonperforming debt to commercial banks. These reforms, however, proved insufficient for two main reasons. First, they could not prevent the accumulation of further losses by public enterprises, given that many of these enterprises could not set their prices freely but continued to enjoy easy access to commercial bank credit. Second, reforms did not involve the physical restructuring of public enterprises. From 1994, these shortcomings were addressed mainly by subjecting all public enterprises to harder budget constraints. Moreover, for the 23 largest loss-marketing enterprises that accounted for close to 15 percent of the value added in industry and construction, a ceiling was imposed on their access to commercial bank credit, while medium-term plans were drawn to cut operating losses by imposing better inventory control and cost management procedures. In addition, to improve competitiveness, labor costs were reduced and production was reoriented toward more viable activities. By the end of 1996, all 23 enterprises had been granted autonomy in conjunction with the completing of their financial restructuring and the signing of performance contracts with their managers. Furthermore, in September 1996, the commercial banks and the 11 holdings that now group all the large public enterprises established financial programs aimed at restoring the financial viability of the large public enterprises and closing the nonviable ones.

Progress was also achieved toward the restructuring of other public enterprises. In 1995, a program was launched to privatize, downsize, or liquidate all public construction companies. This entailed the dissolution of 19 enterprises and the layoff of more than 25 percent of the initial workforce. Retrenchment was facilitated by the introduction, in July 1994, of a new unemployment insurance system providing for lump-sum severance payments to dismissed workers (see Section VI). Over 1994–97, the government also undertook debt conversion operations to clean up the balance sheets of food-importing agencies, utility companies, and public real estate management companies. These public entities also received cash transfers from the Rehabilitation Fund, which was established by the 1991 budget law and liquidated at the end of 1996 to ensure the end of government bailouts (with all payments ending in March 1997).

The process of government disengagement from productive activities called for the adoption of a comprehensive legal framework to privatize public enterprises and foster private investment. The 1994 complementary budget law allowed for the first time the sale of public enterprises, the offer of public enterprises for private management contracts, and the private participation of up to 49 percent in the equity of public enterprises. The legal framework was further extended by the 1995 privatization law, which allowed 100 percent private ownership in most public enterprises. Furthermore, in 1994, the government approved a law removing the state's monopoly in the insurance market and amended the 1994 Investment Code to allow foreign participation in the capital of commercial banks. In addition, a law promulgated in 1995 restored to original owners certain lands that had been nationalized after independence. Finally, to enhance the efficiency of agriculture, the government adopted in early 1997 a draft law to transform into full-fledged property rights the usufruct rights granted to farmers in 1988, at the time of the dismantling of socialist farms. Legislative approval of this measure—still pending in 1998—would facilitate farmers' access to bank credit and hence investment in agriculture.

Within this framework, in April 1996, a first privatization program was launched with World Bank support, targeting about 200 small local public enterprises, mostly in the service sector. However, it was only in late 1996, after the creation of five regional holdings, that the dismantling and privatization process gained momentum. Indeed, as of April 1998, more than 800 local enterprises had been privatized or dissolved. Moreover, at the end of 1997, a second privatization program focusing on large public enterprises was adopted, covering about 250 enterprises

III MACROECONOMIC STABILIZATION AND STRUCTURAL REFORMS

to be sold over 1998–99. To facilitate the effective privatization of these enterprises and to address the problem posed by the relative scarcity of private domestic savings, the 1995 law was amended in April 1997 to introduce more flexibility in divestment procedures—opening the possibility of payment in installments, equity participation by employees, and voucher privatization.

Beyond these privatization initiatives, new institutions were established to promote private sector development. In particular, a national investment agency was set up in 1994 to act as a one-stop window to help private investors, domestic and foreign, cut through bureaucratic red tape and administer tax breaks and other investment incentives. In the construction sector, contracts have been increasingly awarded to the private sector by breaking up the size of contracts previously awarded to public construction companies.

Significant headway has been made since 1994 in the area of financial sector reform to improve the efficiency of financial intermediation and to safeguard the soundness of the banking system. In addition to the emergence of real positive interest rates since the beginning of 1996, the financial viability of Algeria's five state-owned banks was strengthened by their recapitalization and the swap of government bonds for nonperforming bank loans to public enterprises. On this basis, banks have begun to adopt more competitive behavior while being subject to strengthened prudential regulations (see Section V).

IV Fiscal Policy

The transformation of Algeria from a centrally planned economy to a market economy was accompanied by a major reorientation of the government's fiscal policy. Under the central planning system, fiscal policy focused mainly on allocating the rent extracted from hydrocarbon exports to maintain a large civil service, provide generalized transfers and subsidies, for both consumption and production, and undertake large nonpriority public investment projects. With the emergence of a market economy, the government endeavored to limit its role to the provision of public goods and services. In addition, the budget assumed a major role in the stabilization process by bringing about macroeconomic stability and releasing resources to the private sector through fiscal consolidation. On the structural side, the budget was strengthened by recasting the tax system to gradually reduce the dependence on hydrocarbon revenue and by reorienting expenditures to growth-promoting areas such as education and health, while improving the targeting of social safety nets to protect the most vulnerable groups from the costs of adjustment.

Attempts at Fiscal Adjustment Prior to 1994

Before 1986, notwithstanding favorable oil prices, Algeria had already experienced substantial fiscal deficits, which reflected mainly net lending to finance public enterprise investment. In 1986, these fiscal weaknesses were exacerbated when hydrocarbon revenue, which provided about one-half of total budget revenue, fell by more than 50 percent as a result of the drop in world oil prices without any countervailing exchange rate adjustment (Figure 2). This revenue contraction, only partially offset by a reduction in capital expenditure and net lending, resulted in a widening of the overall deficit from 10.7 percent of GDP in 1985 to 13.7 percent of GDP in 1988.

The persistence of large fiscal imbalances and the associated buildup of external debt prompted the government to undertake a more forceful fiscal adjustment in the context of the two IMF-supported programs of 1989 and 1991. This adjustment, coupled with a sharp increase in oil prices in the wake of the 1990–91 crisis, resulted in a surplus of 1.7 percent of GDP in 1991 (Table 4). On the revenue side, hydrocarbon revenue rose by about 12 percentage points of GDP between 1988 and 1991. The bulk of this increase, 9 percentage points of GDP, represented the impact of the depreciation of the Algerian dinar, while the remaining 3 percentage points resulted from higher world oil prices. Nonhydrocarbon revenue declined by nearly 7 percentage points of GDP, largely reflecting the poor performance of public enterprises and the contraction of profits transferred from the Bank of Algeria, stemming in part from its exchange rate losses on external debt. As a result of these divergent trends, the structure of budgetary revenues changed dramatically, increasing the share of hydrocarbon revenue in total revenue from 23 percent in 1985 to about 58 percent in 1993.

On the expenditure side, a tight incomes policy and further cuts in investment outlays helped to reduce budgetary expenditure by 6 percentage points of GDP between 1998 and 1991. In particular, capital expenditure fell from 12.4 percent of GDP in 1988 to 6.2 percent of GDP in 1991. The contraction was particularly pronounced for education and economic infrastructure (see Figure 3). In addition, net lending was substantially curtailed, as legislation was introduced to halt treasury financing of new investments by public enterprises and of public housing for rent. These savings more than compensated for additional spending arising from two elements: (1) the increased cost of generalized consumption subsidies owing to the impact of exchange rate depreciation, and (2) the launching of a major restructuring program for public enterprises with the assistance of the World Bank Enterprise and Financial Sector Adjustment Loan. As part of this program, the 1991 budget law established a fund for the financial rehabilitation of public enterprises and banks. In 1991, this fund channeled 2.6 percent of GDP to recapitalize banks and public enterprises.[3]

---

[3]Disbursements of the Rehabilitation Fund also compensated for foreign exchange losses incurred mainly by state-owned banks on past external borrowing to import basic food staples and other consumer goods at the behest of the government. This compensation is registered among the financing items of the budget.

IV FISCAL POLICY

Table 4. Summary of Central Government Operations

	1986	1987	1988	1989	1990	1991	1992	1993	1994	1995	1996	1997
	(In billions of Algerian dinars)											
Total budget revenue and grants	92.3	93.1	93.5	120.9	160.2	272.4	316.8	320.1	434.2	600.9	824.8	926.7
Hydrocarbon revenue	21.4	20.5	24.1	45.5	76.2	161.5	201.3	185.0	257.7	358.8	519.7	592.5
Nonhydrocarbon revenue	70.9	72.6	69.4	75.4	84.0	110.9	115.5	135.1	176.5	242.1	305.1	334.2
Tax revenue	54.5	58.1	58.1	69.0	78.8	106.2	109.1	126.1	163.2	233.2	290.5	314.0
Taxes												
On income and profits	19.5	19.8	20.9	21.9	21.6	22.5	28.1	35.0	42.8	53.6	67.5	81.8
On goods and services[1]	27.8	28.8	28.2	35.1	42.4	61.7	48.4	54.2	65.9	99.9	129.5	148.1
Customs duties	5.1	7.1	6.1	8.4	11.3	18.5	27.3	30.0	47.9	73.3	84.4	73.5
Registration and stamps	2.1	2.4	2.9	3.6	3.5	3.5	5.3	6.9	6.6	6.4	9.1	10.6
Nontax revenues	16.4	14.5	11.3	6.4	5.2	4.7	6.4	9.0	13.3	8.9	14.6	20.2
Grants	0.0	0.0	0.0	0.0	0.0	0.0	0.0	0.0	0.0	0.0	0.0	0.0
Total budget expenditure	107.8	105.3	121.3	125.6	142.5	239.6	308.7	390.5	461.9	589.1	724.6	845.2
Current expenditure	66.2	67.0	77.9	83.1	96.9	187.6	236.1	288.9	344.7	444.4	550.6	643.6
Personnel expenditure	31	37.0	39.5	45.2	51.4	71.0	100.0	121.5	151.7	187.5	222.8	245.2
Mudjahidins' pensions	...	...	...	3.5	4.1	5.9	6.4	10.0	12.8	15.6	18.9	25.0
Material and supplies	2.8	2.6	2.9	3.4	3.8	8.1	12.1	16.7	18.2	29.4	34.7	43.6
Current transfers	23	20.5	23.7	23.8	28.6	87.0	94.5	113.7	120.9	149.7	185.2	220.5
Of which:												
Compensation Fund[2]	2.5	1.3	1.7	2.8	10.2	47.5	52.2	57.4	42.4	25.5	18.8	6.0
Debt service	9.4	6.9	11.8	7.2	9.0	15.6	23.1	27.0	41.1	62.2	89.0	109.4
Capital expenditure	41.6	38.3	43.4	42.5	45.6	52.0	72.6	101.6	117.2	144.7	174.0	201.6
Special accounts balance	−5.3	1.7	0.8	4.0	1.8	3.5	12.6	5.6	1.1	−0.7	1.5	1.1
Net lending by the treasury	17.6	16.1	20.8	6.7	−0.7	0.2	9.2	11.5	7.0	2.4	2.4	−1.5
Rehabilitation Fund[3]	0	0.0	0.0	0.0	0.0	21.8	23.7	24.3	31.7	36.9	24.4	18.0
Primary balance[4]	−29.0	−19.7	−36.0	−0.2	29.2	29.9	10.9	−73.6	−24.3	34.0	163.9	175.5
Overall balance	−38.4	−26.6	−47.8	−7.4	20.2	14.3	−12.2	−100.6	−65.4	−28.2	74.9	66.1
Financing	38.4	26.6	47.8	7.4	−20.2	−14.3	12.2	100.6	65.4	28.2	−74.9	−66.1
Bank[5]	24.4	15.7	23.7	6.0	−16.5	−14.0	11.5	72.8	−99.8	−106.6	−140.1	−99.0
Nonbank	13.9	10.2	23.1	0.9	−4.0	5.6	−12.7	8.2	41.8	−14.7	−7.4	−23.1
Foreign[6]	0.1	0.7	1.0	0.5	0.3	−5.9	13.4	19.6	123.4	149.5	72.6	56.0
	(In percent of GDP)											
Total revenue	32.3	30.5	26.7	28.6	28.8	32.3	30.3	27.6	29.5	30.4	33.0	34.0
Hydrocarbon revenue	7.5	6.7	6.9	10.8	13.7	19.1	19.3	15.9	17.5	18.2	20.8	21.8
Nonhydrocarbon	24.8	23.8	19.8	17.8	15.1	13.1	11.1	11.6	12.0	12.3	12.2	12.3
Tax revenue	19.1	19.0	16.6	16.3	14.2	12.6	10.4	10.9	11.1	11.8	11.6	11.5
Total expenditure	37.7	34.5	34.7	29.7	25.6	28.4	29.5	33.6	31.4	29.8	29.0	31.0
Current expenditure	23.2	21.9	22.3	19.7	17.4	22.2	22.6	24.9	23.4	22.5	22.0	23.6
Personnel expenditure	10.8	12.1	11.3	10.7	9.2	8.4	9.6	10.5	10.3	9.5	8.9	9.0

Attempts at Fiscal Adjustment Prior to 1994

	\multicolumn{11}{c}{(In percent of GDP)}
Current transfers	8.0	6.7	6.8	5.6	5.1	10.3	9.0	9.8	8.2	7.6	7.4	8.1
Of which:												
Compensation Fund[2]	0.9	0.4	0.5	0.7	1.8	5.6	5.0	4.9	2.9	1.3	0.8	0.2
Debt service	3.3	2.3	3.4	1.7	1.6	1.8	2.2	2.3	2.8	3.1	3.6	4.0
Capital expenditure	14.6	12.5	12.4	10.1	8.2	6.2	6.9	8.7	8.0	7.3	7.0	7.4
Net lending	6.2	5.3	5.9	1.6	-0.1	0.0	0.9	1.0	0.5	0.1	0.1	-0.1
Rehabilitation and recapitalization	0.0	0.0	0.0	0.0	0.0	2.6	2.3	2.1	2.2	1.9	1.0	0.7
Primary balance	-10.1	-6.4	-10.3	0.0	5.3	3.5	1.0	-6.3	-1.7	1.7	6.5	6.4
Overall balance	-13.4	-8.7	-13.7	-1.8	3.6	1.7	-1.2	-8.7	-4.4	-1.4	3.0	2.4

(In billions of Algerian dinars, unless otherwise indicated)

Memorandum items:												
GDP at current prices	286	306	350	423	556	844	1,045	1,162	1,471	1,966	2,495	2,716
Crude oil price (in U.S. dollars/barrel)	14.9	18.6	16.2	18.6	24.3	20.4	20.1	17.8	16.3	17.6	21.7	19.8
Exchange rate (average)	4.7	4.9	5.9	7.6	9.0	18.7	21.8	23.3	35.1	47.7	54.8	57.8

Sources: Algerian authorities; and IMF staff estimates.
[1]Including excise duties on petroleum products.
[2]Covers expenditures for food subsidies, agricultural price support, and cash transfers to the poor. Expenditures under the new public works program are not included.
[3]Excluding the compensation for commercial banks' foreign exchange losses on principal payments of external debt.
[4]Including special accounts, net lending, and operations of the Rehabilitation Fund.
[5]Including debt rescheduling proceeds blocked on account at the Bank of Algeria.
[6]Includes external debt rescheduling proceeds.

IV FISCAL POLICY

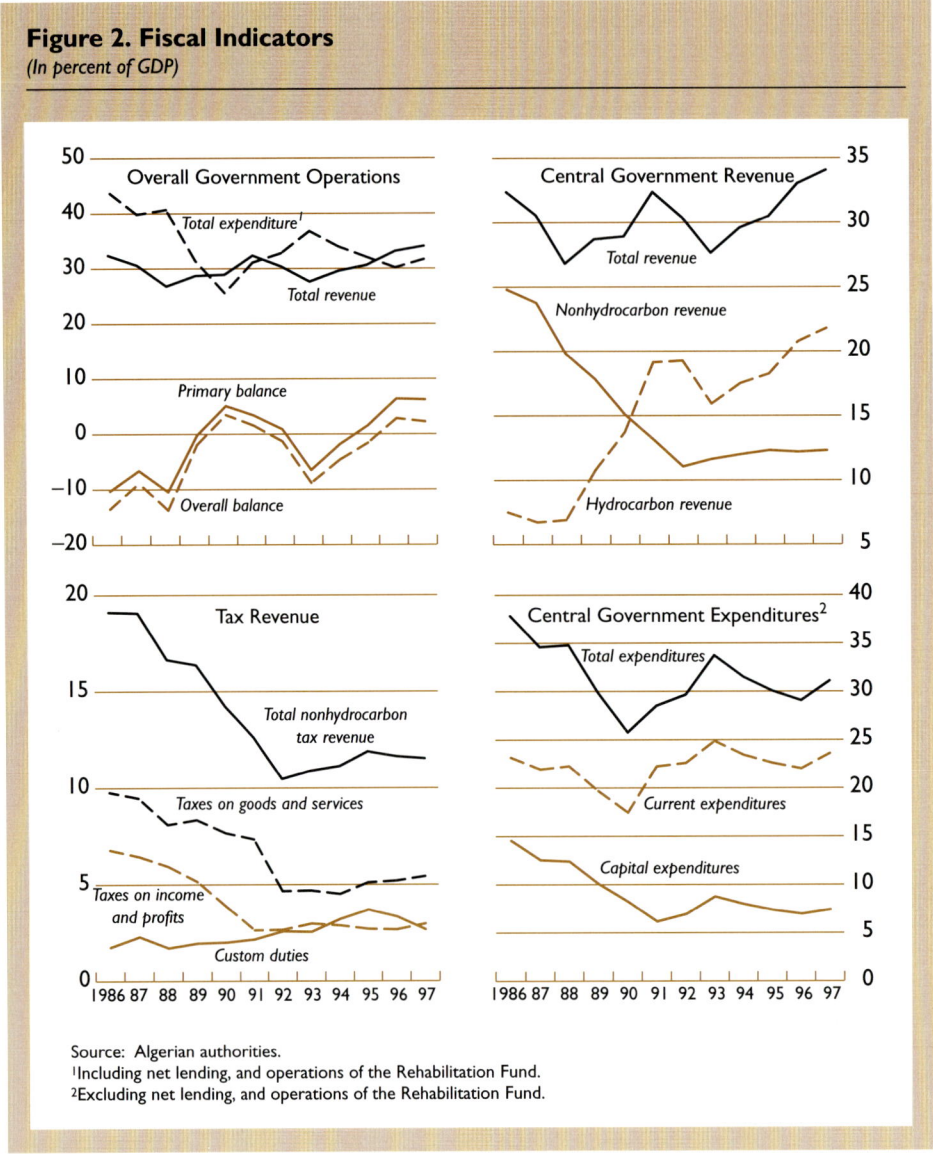

Figure 2. Fiscal Indicators
(In percent of GDP)

Source: Algerian authorities.
[1]Including net lending, and operations of the Rehabilitation Fund.
[2]Excluding net lending, and operations of the Rehabilitation Fund.

Notwithstanding the adjustment in the overall balance, expenditure control weakened during 1989–91, and, as a result, budgetary arrears increased.

Progress in fiscal consolidation during the first phase of the adjustment was set back in 1992–93 when fiscal discipline was relaxed against the backdrop of civil strife. In particular, wages in the central administration were increased by more than 20 percent a year, raising the government wage bill by more than 2 percentage points of GDP between 1991 and 1993. Moreover, in an attempt to stimulate economic growth, the authorities increased capital expenditure and net lending by 3.5 percentage points of GDP. The negative effect of these expenditure increases on the fiscal balance was exacerbated by a weak revenue performance even though, in 1992, additional taxes were introduced as part of an important reform of the tax system (see Box 1). Hydrocarbon revenue suffered from an overvalued exchange rate and unfavorable oil prices, while nonhydrocarbon budget revenue declined mainly owing to the import compression brought about by the introduction of an array of trade and payment restrictions, and the adverse impact of this compression on economic activity. Overall, the fiscal balance deteriorated from a surplus of 1.7 percent of GDP in 1991 to a deficit of 8.7 percent of GDP in 1993.

Fiscal Adjustment Since 1994

Substantial fiscal consolidation was achieved from 1994 onward, and the overall fiscal balance

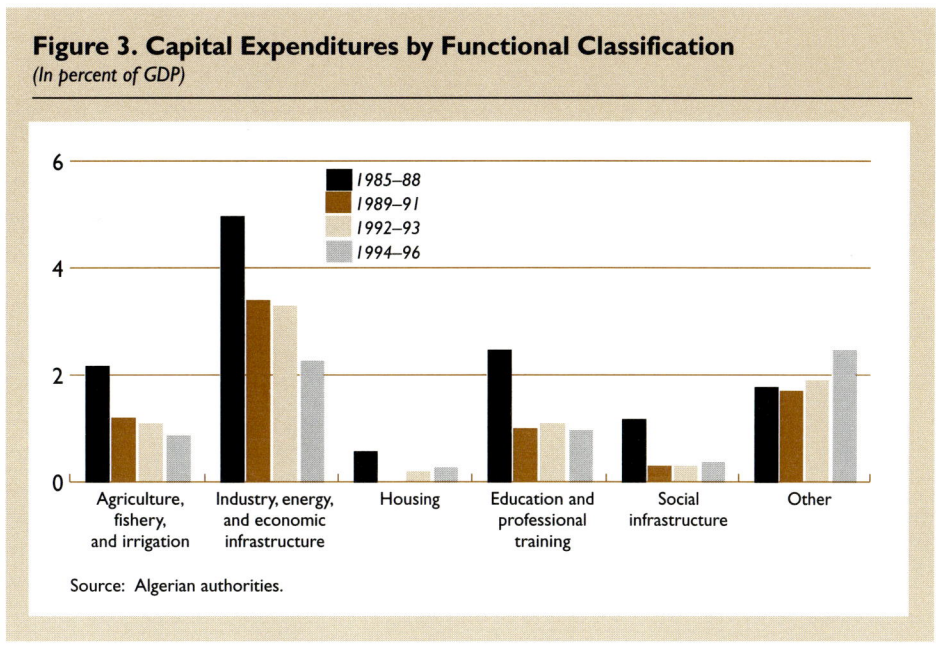

Figure 3. Capital Expenditures by Functional Classification
(In percent of GDP)

Source: Algerian authorities.

shifted from a deficit equivalent to 8.7 percent of GDP in 1993 to a surplus of 2.4 percent of GDP in 1997. The extent of fiscal adjustment is even more striking when measured in terms of the primary balance, which improved by 12.7 percentage points of GDP over the same period. Beyond the reduction in government absorption, the adjustment program implemented since 1994 succeeded in virtually eliminating the sources of quasi-fiscal deficits and increasing the ability of the Ministry of Finance over the medium term to use tax and expenditure policies as an efficient tool of macroeconomic management, thereby making the fiscal balance less vulnerable to fluctuations in world oil prices (Figure 4).

Revenue Developments

Between 1993 and 1997, budget revenues, which continued to be highly dependent on hydrocarbon receipts, increased by about 6 percentage points of GDP. This strong performance was the consequence of several key elements in Algeria's adjustment program, including (1) the realignment of the exchange rate; (2) the increase in imports brought about by trade liberalization; and (3) the implementation of measures to strengthen the tax system and broaden the tax base.

Hydrocarbon revenues, in Algerian dinar terms, were more than three times higher in 1997 than they were in 1993. The bulk of this increase (75 percent) was due to the exchange rate depreciation. Hydrocarbon revenues were also boosted in 1997 by the increase in the world price of crude oil by up to $4 a barrel in 1996, remaining at that level in 1997, and by higher export volumes (7.6 percent). In addition, a mechanism was established to adjust the price of crude oil sold by the national oil company, Sonatrach, to domestic refineries in line with the evolution of world prices. This mechanism strengthened Sonatrach's financial position and allowed the company to distribute higher dividends to the government. Overall, the increase in hydrocarbon budget receipts represented about 50 percent of the fiscal consolidation over 1993–97.

Nonhydrocarbon revenues as a share of GDP recovered from their low levels of 1992–93 mainly owing to the good performance of trade-related taxes. Custom duties and valued-added tax (VAT) on imports rebounded as a result of higher import volumes and the exchange rate depreciation as well as the removal of several exemptions and reduction of tariff dispersion. Nonhydrocarbon taxes registered at about a 1 percentage point improvement as a share of GDP from 1993 to 1997, despite the following improvements in the tax system: (1) an increase of the tax rate on reinvested profits from 5 percent to 33 percent; (2) a change in taxation for petroleum products consumed domestically; and (3) the reduction in exemptions on VAT, the increase in the VAT rates, and an increase in the central government's share in VAT proceeds.[4] The stagnation of the ratio of nonhydrocarbon taxes to GDP reflects the decline of the share of nonhydrocarbon GDP in total GDP owing partly to

---

[4]The central government's share in VAT proceeds amounts to 85 percent of the total, and the remaining 15 percent accrues to local governments.

IV FISCAL POLICY

Box 1. Tax Reforms

In the early 1990s, Algeria had a complex and highly distorted tax system stemming from ad hoc measures introduced since independence to adapt the colonial tax system to a centrally planned economy. This system was substantially simplified and improved by the 1992 tax reform. Since then, other reforms have corrected some problems associated with the design of the new tax regime and introduced additional taxes in accordance with the needs of a market economy.

The 1992 reform improved both direct and indirect taxation.

- Concerning direct taxes, a new corporate tax on all profits replaced several schedular taxes. In 1992, two main rates of taxation existed: 42 percent on profits distributed to shareholders and 5 percent on retained earnings. They were supplemented by seven other rates specific to some activities and many exemptions applied. Similarly, a unified personal income tax replaced a system of several schedular taxes and a surtax. The new tax scale, despite its 12 rates ranging from zero to 70 percent, provided a significant tax relief with respect to the previous system. In addition, a property tax was introduced together with official guidelines concerning the assessment of property values.

- Concerning indirect taxes, the crucial element of the reform was the introduction of a value-added tax (VAT) with four rates ranging from zero to 40 percent. The VAT was simpler than the previous indirect tax system and allowed for a larger tax base, a substantial reduction in the highest rates, and the elimination of cumulative taxation, in particular for services. Some activities or sectors, such as exports, retail sales, agriculture, banking and insurance, and liberal professions, were not subject to VAT.

The 1992 tax reform was supplemented by the implementation of a new custom tariff of eight rates, ranging from zero to 60 percent. While the new tariff provided for a significantly higher taxation of finished products compared to the taxation of raw materials and intermediate goods, its introduction greatly reduced differences between the highest and lowest rates and allowed for the integration of a large portion of the compensatory tax[1] in the tariff structure.

Since 1993, reforms have aimed mainly at improving the structure of the tax system introduced in 1992, in particular through the following measures:

- A new Investment Code introduced, in 1993, a special treatment for investment in specific areas as well as a general regime granting tax benefits to both resident and nonresident investors for all sectors not specifically reserved to the state;

- A wealth tax was introduced by the budget law for 1993 to replace a solidarity tax on real estate;

- Individual and corporate income tax rates were restructured in 1994 to reduce the incidence of taxation and increase the tax base. In particular, the corporate tax rate was reduced from 42 percent to 38 percent (33 percent for reinvested profits) while the marginal rate for the personal income tax was reduced from 70 percent to 50 percent;

- Excise taxes were introduced in 1994 on luxury goods;

- The VAT was simplified in 1995 by eliminating the highest rate of 40 percent, leaving the maximum at 21 percent, and its coverage was progressively extended to include the banking and insurance sectors, professional activities, and petroleum products. In addition, as of January 1997, the rate of 13 percent was increased to 14 percent and a number of products subject to the special rate of 7 percent were shifted to the 14 percent rate.

- The import tariff was restructured in 1996 and 1997. The number of rates was reduced to five, ranging from zero to 45 percent.

---
[1] An earmarked levy on imports and domestic production that provided resources for the Compensation Fund, an extrabudgetary fund in charge of administering consumption and production subsidies. This tax was eliminated by the 1994 budget law.

---

the recent increase in the relative price of oil on world markets and partly to the decline in manufacturing activity and related services. When measured in terms of nonhydrocarbon GDP, the tax effort increased between 1993 and 1997. Nevertheless, in the case of Algeria, nonhydrocarbon GDP is only a proxy for the tax base for nonhydrocarbon taxes (see Box 2).

Expenditure Developments

Between 1993 and 1997, budgetary expenditures decreased by about 5 percentage points of GDP. This significant reduction, which affected both current and capital expenditures, reflected several policy actions undertaken to reduce expenditures—while improving their composition and transparency—including a tight incomes policy, price liberalization, and a better prioritization of public investment projects. Part of the savings from these actions was used to eliminate quasi-fiscal deficits and to reinforce the social safety net.

Current expenditures were reduced by 3.5 percentage points of GDP between 1993 and 1997, as a tight cap was imposed on most spending items despite the exchange rate depreciation and its impact

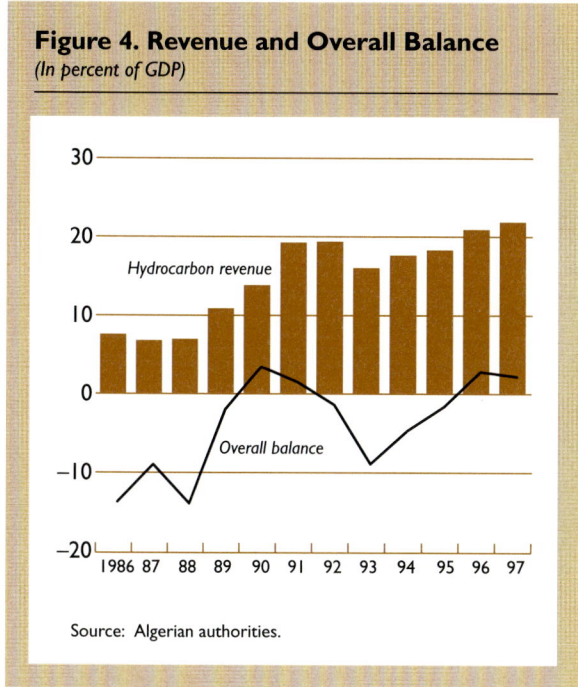

Figure 4. Revenue and Overall Balance
(In percent of GDP)

Source: Algerian authorities.

on domestic prices. Personnel expenditure, which accounted for one-third of total expenditures in 1993, declined by 1.4 percentage points of GDP by 1997 in response to both a strict wage policy and a freeze on the size of the civil service (see Box 3). Important budgetary savings were also realized on current transfers mainly as a result of the elimination of generalized subsidies on basic food and petroleum products and the reduction of producer subsidies in the agricultural sector. In addition, spending on the social safety net was made more efficient through improved targeting (see Section VI). These savings offset the higher budgetary appropriations for interest payments, mostly on account of the impact of the exchange rate depreciation on external debt service (Figure 5). Moreover, with the objective of eventually eliminating quasi-fiscal deficits, implicit subsidies to the national gas and electricity company and the railroads were made explicit in the budget. At the same time, all expenditures for new public housing were incorporated into the budget instead of being financed through the public housing bank (Box 4).

After their surge in 1993, capital expenditures and net lending were reduced by about 2.4 percent of GDP by 1997, notwithstanding the rise in investment costs caused by the Algerian dinar depreciation and the spending required to repair infrastructures damaged by civil strife. The large decline in capital expenditure in real terms also reflected a recognition of the low social rate of return of past investment. As for the reduction in net lending, it was mainly due to the de-

crease in the number of public enterprises' investment projects, which were still partly financed through the budget because they had been launched prior to 1988.

Fiscal consolidation over 1994–97 also reflected the winding down of cash transfers channeled through the Rehabilitation Fund from 2.1 percent of GDP in 1993 to 0.7 percent of GDP in 1997. This reflected the government's commitment to avoid recurrent bailouts of public enterprises and banks by accompanying financial restructuring with structural measures, including price liberalization and labor shedding. In addition, managers were made increasingly responsible for finding alternative financial resources for enterprise restructuring, such as sales of assets, capitalization from partnerships, and bank credit. This commitment culminated in the closure of the Rehabilitation Fund at the end of 1996 (though some disbursements still took place in early 1997). Beyond cash transfers, enterprise restructuring and the elimination of quasi-fiscal deficits resulted in a swap of government bonds for nonperforming bank loans to public real estate management agencies. This operation took place in 1995 and amounted to DA 92 billion (about 4.7 percentage points of GDP).[5] Furthermore, government bonds worth 1 percent of GDP were issued in 1996 to recapitalize commercial banks.

Despite these operations, the stock of domestic government debt decreased from about 45 percent of GDP in 1993 to about 22 percent of GDP in 1997. Beyond the fiscal surplus achieved in 1997, this reduction in domestic indebtedness was made possible by the availability of large amounts of foreign financing arising from the monetization of part of the external debt rescheduling proceeds. When both domestic and external obligations are taken into account, the stock of public debt decreased from 99 percent of GDP in 1993 to about 85 percent of GDP in 1997, despite the impact of the depreciation of the Algerian dinar.

Remaining Agenda for Fiscal Consolidation and Reform

To build upon its successful fiscal consolidation, Algeria faces several important challenges: (1) to maintain fiscal discipline in the face of expenditure pressures arising inter alia from high interest payments and growing social needs, such as in public housing; (2) to avoid the reemergence of quasi-fiscal deficits; (3) to

---

[5]A similar operation of DA 187 billion (about 7 percent of GDP) took place in early 1997 to clean up the balance sheet of the food-importing agencies, the gas and electricity company, and the railway company.

IV FISCAL POLICY

Box 2. Tax Effort in Algeria: Looking at the Denominator

Is GDP a good measure of the tax base in an open economy? A common indicator used to evaluate a country's tax effort in IMF programs is the ratio of government tax revenue to GDP at market prices. This denominator measures the market value of final goods produced in a country, or alternatively the sum of factor rewards (wages, profits, and rents) generated by domestic production plus indirect taxes. The use of GDP as a measure of the tax base for both direct and indirect taxes is justified in a closed economy. In such an environment, in fact, GDP equals income, which is the tax base for direct taxes, and absorption on which indirect taxes are levied.

In an open economy, however, the identity between product, income, and absorption ceases to apply and, therefore, using GDP as a proxy for the tax base, direct and indirect, can distort the analysis of the tax effort. This is so for two reasons. First, income can differ significantly from GDP because of net factor income and net transfers from abroad. Therefore, in an open economy, gross national disposable income (GNDI) may be a more appropriate measure of the tax base for direct taxes. Second, the sum of absorption and exports, on which indirect taxes are levied, can differ substantially from GDP depending on the importance of imports both in production and in consumption.

Thus, when GDP differs significantly from GNDI, or when imports are substantial, the standard analysis of tax effort on the basis of the tax to GDP ratio should be complemented by the calculation of two additional indicators, namely the ratio of direct taxes to GNDI at factor cost and the ratio of indirect taxes on absorption plus exports. These complementary measures would be all the more useful when exogenous shocks (e.g., changes in the terms of trade or in foreign financing) affect substantially the difference between the GDP and national disposable income.

How does this apply to Algeria, an economy with a substantial mineral rent? The hydrocarbon sector represents the central pillar of the Algerian economy. In 1996, it accounted for nearly 30 percent of GDP and contributed to 95 percent of export receipts and 62 percent of government budgetary revenues. How does such a high dependence on hydrocarbon export receipts affect the manner in which we analyze the tax effort beyond hydrocarbon budgetary revenues?

In a country like Algeria, neither GDP nor nonhydrocarbon GDP is an appropriate measure to evaluate nonhydrocarbon taxes. There are two main shortcomings in using total GDP. First, it includes the rent from the hydrocarbon sector that goes to the government budget as hydrocarbon revenue and is not part of the tax base for nonhydrocarbon direct taxes.[1] Second, GDP does not include imports on which custom duties are levied and it includes oil and other exports, which are obviously exempt from indirect taxes. As for nonhydrocarbon GDP, it provides only a partial measure of nonhydrocarbon income because it excludes net factor income and net transfers from abroad. In addition, similarly to total GDP, it excludes imports and includes exports. The evolution of the ratios of nonhydrocarbon taxes to GDP and nonhydrocarbon GDP between 1994 and 1996 is shown in the table below. To evaluate the Algerian nonhydrocarbon tax effort in 1994–96, the ratio of income taxes over nonhydrocarbon GNDI at factor costs and the ratio of indirect taxes over domestic absorption have also been calculated:

	1994	1995	1996
	(In percent)		
Nonhydrocarbon taxes/GDP	11.1	11.9	11.6
Nonhydrocarbon taxes/ nonhydrocarbon GDP	14.5	16.5	17.1
Income taxes/ nonhyrocarbon GNDI	4.1	4.1	4.3
Income tax/GDP	2.9	2.7	2.7
Indirect taxes/absorption[1]	8.0	9.0	9.9
Indirect taxes/GDP	7.8	8.8	8.6

[1]Imports of the state oil company are excluded from absorption because they are tax exempt. Exports are excluded from the denominator because they are not taxed in Algeria.

While the ratio of nonhydrocarbon taxes to GDP decreased from 1995 to 1996, the two complementary measures reveal that Algeria's tax effort continued to increase over the same period reflecting sustained improvement in tax administration. Not only does GDP as a proxy for the tax base understate the actual tax ratio, but it may be misleading as to the direction and extent of the tax effort.

---

[1]Hydrocarbon GDP includes a small amount of salaries that can be assumed away to simplify the analysis. The feedback into the income stream of government expenditure from hydrocarbon revenue is fully captured by nonhydrocarbon GDP.

Box 3. Government Wage Expenditure, 1985–96

General government wage expenditure[1] averaged 12.7 percent of GDP over 1980–85 before reaching a peak of more than 16 percent of GDP in 1988 as a result of the introduction of a new salary scale in the civil service in 1986 and the reverse oil shock. This trend was reversed in 1989–90, when the government wage bill was brought down to 14.2 percent of GDP on account of the tight fiscal policy pursued during Algeria's first IMF-supported program. This share continued to decline in 1991 despite a substantial increase in the government wage bill owing to the pass-through effect of the exchange rate devaluation on the GDP deflator. It started to rise again in 1992–93 owing to the relaxation of fiscal policy, compounded with the impact of weak oil prices and the increasing overvaluation of the Algerian dinar. Expenditure restraint, which has constituted a major element of Algeria's stabilization program since 1994, has reduced the share of government wages in GDP to 11.2 percent in 1996. This share is marginally less than the 11.5 percent prevailing in Morocco and Tunisia. It remains well above the share of about 5 percent prevailing in some east Asian developing countries such as Thailand and the Philippines.

The evolution of government wage expenditures reflects employment and incomes policies. Civil service staff increased at an average of 3.3 percent a year from 1985 to 1995, with a slowdown in the 1990s. This slowdown has, however, been limited by the need to hire security personnel in the face of civil strife. As a result, government employment has continued to grow faster than the total population, and the size of the civil service, per hundred inhabitants, increased from 4.1 in 1985 to 4.4 in 1995. This level is more than the weighted average of less than 3 calculated for Jordan, Morocco, the Syrian Arab Republic, and Tunisia, which in turn is well above the weighted average of about 2.3 calculated for Indonesia, Korea, the Philippines, Singapore, Malaysia, and Thailand. The growth of the Algerian civil service is even more apparent when measured as a ratio of government employment to total employment, which rose from 23.4 percent in 1985 to 28 percent in 1995. Several steps were taken in 1996 toward reversing this trend, including a freeze in net recruitment and a strict enforcement of the retirement age at 60.

In 1986, despite the 50 percent fall in Algeria's terms of trade, a new salary scale was introduced in the civil service resulting in an increase in nominal wages of about 14 percent including drift.[2] The government's wage policy was subsequently tightened, particularly in the context of the 1989 IMF-supported adjustment program. In 1990, however, the average government wage rose again by more than 10 percent owing to a general wage increase and new bonuses for workers with special skills. Incomes policy continued to be relaxed in 1991 and 1992 on account of a wage agreement concluded in December 1991 before the parliamentary elections. As a result, government wages increased on average by about 30 percent a year during this period. In 1993, despite a formal salary freeze, additional benefits were granted, thereby increasing the role of allowances in the government incomes policy. A major tightening of incomes policy has occurred in the context of Algeria's ongoing adjustment program, as the general wage in the civil service was only increased twice by 10 percent between March 1994 and the end of 1996. As a result, real government wages fell by more than 30 percent from 1994 to 1996, whereas they had declined by less than 4 percent between 1985 and 1993.

---

[1] General employment includes central and local governments and public institutions such as universities.

[2] The wage drift in Algeria has been about 3 percent a year over 1985–95. This relatively high level reflects that most of Algeria's government employees are young and in the lower civil service grades.

---

reduce the dependency on hydrocarbon revenues and trade taxes; and (4) to reorient public expenditure so that it can provide the necessary underpinning for private sector-led growth and employment creation.

Over the medium term, Algeria needs to sustain fiscal balance or a small fiscal surplus for two main reasons. First, public finances need to be cushioned against volatility in the world oil prices. In particular, budget surpluses contribute to lower the domestic public debt-to-GDP ratio while allowing the buildup of adequate provisions for future payments on the rescheduled external debt. The government would thus be in a position to weather temporary revenue shocks in the event of lower oil prices. Second, the depletion of nonrenewable hydrocarbon resources would warrant converting part of the hydrocarbon revenue into alternative productive assets, partly by making more resources available for private sector investment—which is expected to constitute the main engine of growth in the future—and partly by constituting an investment fund, as has been done in other oil-producing countries such as Kuwait and Norway.

On the revenue side, authorities should focus efforts on tax reform, as increases in nontax revenues—expected to come primarily from privatization proceeds—are difficult to predict and likely to be short-lived. Fiscal reforms should strive to broaden the domestic tax base and increase the efficiency of the tax system. Notwithstanding the progress achieved in recent years toward the restructuring of the tax system, Algeria's tax base outside the hydrocarbon sector remains narrow as reflected by a ratio of

IV FISCAL POLICY

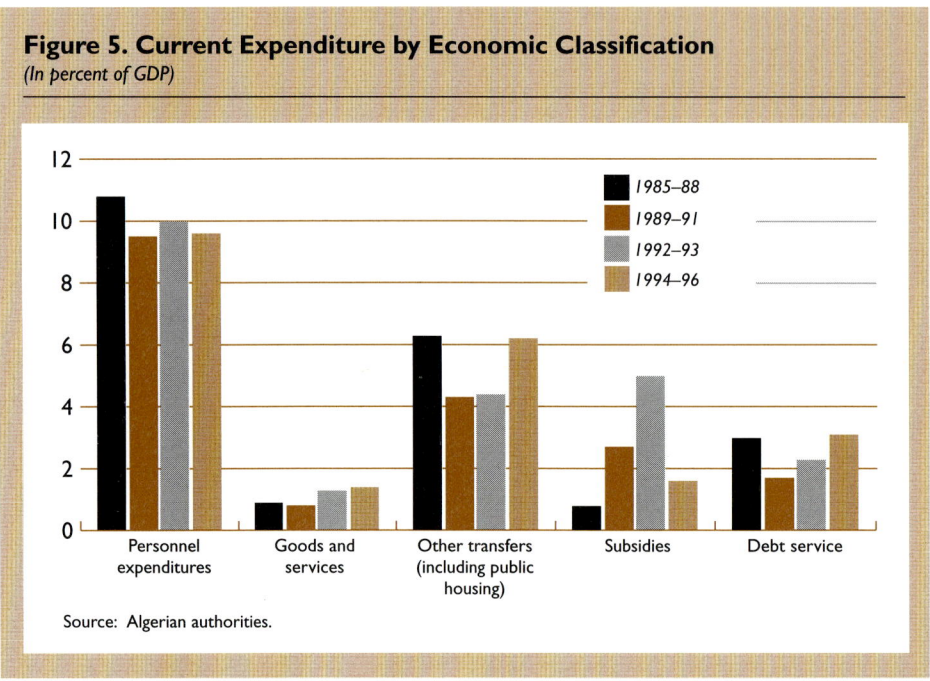

Figure 5. Current Expenditure by Economic Classification
(In percent of GDP)

Source: Algerian authorities.

nonhydrocarbon taxes to GDP that is substantially lower than in neighboring countries (Table 5).

Direct taxes on income and profits are the weakest tax category in Algeria. They are mostly levied on wage earners and, at 2.7 percent of GDP, account for a substantially lower share of revenue than in comparable countries. This share reflects in part the bias introduced by using total GDP as a proxy for the basis tax when it is calculated in terms of nonhydrocarbon disposable income; the ratio rises to 4.1 percent (see Box 2). It also stems from the low profitability of the industrial and construction sectors, which consist mainly of public enterprises in need of further restructuring and privatization. Although profit taxes are expected to improve slowly following a pickup in economic recovery, a strengthening in tax administration will be necessary to ensure tax compliance, in particular by the growing private sector. This will require authorities to establish an effective audit system, and tax return processing and accounting procedures that could detect tax evasion quickly and trigger appropriate actions.

The ratio of customs revenue to GDP in Algeria is broadly in line with levels achieved by most other middle-income countries of the region. However, the need to open the economy to international competition will require further tariff reductions and a consequent decline in trade taxes. In particular, the expected agreement with the European Union on a Free Trade Area will likely involve the phasing out of tariffs on imports from the European Union by 2010. As imports from the European Union account for about two-thirds of Algeria's imports, a Free Trade Area with the European Union would imply a gradual loss of trade-related tax revenue of about 2.5 percentage points of GDP.

In 1995, indirect taxation on nonmineral domestic transactions yielded about 5 percent of GDP compared with an average of almost 8 percent of GDP in comparator countries; only the Syrian Arab Republic and Egypt have lower ratios (Table 5). Narrowing this gap would require enhancing the efficiency of the tax system through further improvements in the VAT system, for instance by reducing the number of rates from three to two. This reduction could increase VAT proceeds and contribute to the elimination of some tax credits. Furthermore, notwithstanding the new taxation introduced in January 1996 on domestically consumed petroleum products, the price of gasoline in Algeria—at about $1.05 a gallon—and those for other petroleum products are still below those prevailing in neighboring countries such as Morocco and Tunisia (Table 6).

On the expenditure side, the authorities ought to be able to achieve further savings without sacrificing the quality of public services. The wage bill could be reduced further by scaling back the excessive size of the civil service and by narrowing the government's involvement in service provision, while strengthening health services in rural areas and the education system to enable it to provide the training and skills that the private sector requires. In addition, there is scope for enhancing efficiency of capital spending at the sectoral level.

> **Box 4. Quasi-Fiscal Deficits: The Algerian Experience**
>
> **Origin of Losses**
>
> Algeria's quasi-fiscal deficits originated primarily from losses of public enterprises and public agencies, reflecting a legacy of state economic planning and the burdening of public enterprises with social objectives.
>
> *Food-importing agencies.* Constrained for many years by a system of administered prices, which did not provide sufficient resources for external debt servicing, food-importing agencies financed their imports through foreign borrowing, assuming the exchange rate risk. The depreciation of the Algerian dinar exacerbated their debt-service obligations, which could not be met with future profits since price increases, made possible by price liberalization, were limited by competing private sector imports. In 1995, the cutoff of external financing forced food-importing agencies to resort to domestic bank credit both to finance large debt repayments—which had been guaranteed by the banks—and ongoing import operations, crowding out other borrowers.
>
> *Public real estate agencies.* Housing is mostly financed by the only mortgage bank, the Caisse nationale d'épargne et de prévoyance (CNEP). Deposits mobilized by the CNEP have to a large extent been lent to public real estate agencies to finance the construction of public housing for rent instead of financing private housing acquisition on commercial terms. Until 1994, the impact of poor rent collection and low levels of rents on the financial situation of the public real estate agencies was partially offset by administered prices imposed on public construction companies, which assumed part of the quasi-fiscal deficits. With the liberalization of construction prices, the public real estate agencies became unable to service their debts to the CNEP, hampering its ability to finance housing construction.
>
> *Gas, electricity, and railroad services.* Sonelgaz and the Société nationale des transports ferroviaires have been providing for many years gas, electricity, and railroad services at administered prices below economic costs. Both enterprises were undercapitalized, and their difficulties were exacerbated by high capital expenditures and the burden of infrastructure maintenance imposed on them by the government. These expenditures and losses were financed by accumulating both domestic and external debt that could not be serviced, particularly after the depreciation of the Algerian dinar.
>
> **Remedies Adopted**
>
> Since 1994, to eliminate these quasi-fiscal deficits, the government has adopted a four-pronged strategy consisting of:
>
> - liberalization of domestic prices and gradual increases in rates and rents toward their equilibrium levels;
> - implementation, in the context of performance contracts, of structural reforms, including the privatization of most food-importing agencies and public real estate agencies;
> - budgeting of any residual subsidy, as well as the maintenance costs of the rail network in the case of Société nationale des transports ferroviaires and rural electrification in the case of Sonelgaz; and
> - swap of DA 279 billion of bank debt, incurred by the food-importing agencies, the public real estate agencies, and utilities for long-term government bonds.

In the past, the civil service was used as an employer of last resort, resulting in overemployment and an excessive wage bill, as well as a disproportionate number of administrative staff compared to specialized staff. A number of years of wage restraint have led to a substantial decline in real wages together with wage compression, and further decline and compression might negatively affect incentives and performance in the civil service. Thus, wages could be selectively raised provided savings were achieved by reducing the number of civil servants. To this end, two main actions would be necessary: (1) a reduction in the number of activities in which the central government is involved by privatization or devolution of some service provision to the private sector; and (2) an increase in the productivity of the civil service, with the adoption of revised salary scales and more modern technology.

At the sectoral level, the most recent Public Expenditure Review conducted in collaboration with the World Bank[6] identifies three main sectors in which policy actions are needed: health, education, and transportation, which together accounted for about 30 percent of total expenditures in 1996. In all these sectors, the adjustment requires a two-pronged strategy. In the short term, increased efficiency could be achieved through (1) better use of existing human resources and physical capacity; (2) redirection of expenditures in favor of maintenance and supplies; and (3) introduction of user's participation in cost-sharing. In the medium term, the challenge will be to limit the role of government and to redirect the provision of public services, particularly education, toward the changing needs of the economy brought about by greater competition and integration with the global economy.

---

[6]World Bank, Algeria: Public Expenditure Review (draft), 1997.

IV FISCAL POLICY

Table 5. Comparative Tax Performance, 1995
(In percent of GDP)

	Algeria	Egypt	Jordan	Morocco	Syrian Arab Republic	Tunisia	Turkey
Tax on income and profits[1]	2.7	3.6	3.3	6.1	4.7	5.7	5.6
Customs duties[2]	3.7	3.5	5.5	4.3	2.4	4.3	0.7
Consumption taxes[3]	5.1	4.6	5.8	11.8	2.2	9.6	7.5
Total	11.5	11.7	14.6	22.2	9.3	19.6	13.8

[1] Excluding rents from petroleum and other mineral resources, and privatization revenue.
[2] Excluding VAT on imports.
[3] All indirect taxes on domestic transactions.

Table 6. International Comparison of Petroleum Products' Prices
(Prices in U.S. dollars per gallon, end-1996)

	International price[1]	Algeria	Egypt	Jordan	Lebanon	Morocco	Tunisia
Gasoline	0.62	1.05	1.10	1.17	0.65	3.14	2.07
Diesel fuel	0.63	0.60	0.39	0.59	0.68	1.88	1.21
Kerosene	0.64	...	0.45	0.48	0.66	1.62	0.78
Fuel oil	0.33	0.60	0.13	...	0.41	0.61	0.70

[1] Ex refinery price in Italy for Mediterranean delivery on a CIF basis.

Increasing the efficiency and effectiveness of government spending would also require an improvement in public expenditure management. As pointed out by the Public Expenditure Review, Algeria's budget law still has limited coverage; in particular, it excludes the treasury's special accounts operations. Furthermore, the budget presentation does not provide for a consistent treatment of current spending (which is broken down by ministry) and capital expenditure (which follows a sectoral breakdown). In addition, the budget preparation process has suffered from several shortcomings such as insufficient coordination between the preparation of the current budget, for which the Ministry of Finance is responsible, and the investment budget,[7] for which the Ministry of Planning is responsible; and the lack of a medium-term framework to guide the allocation of budget resources among ministries. Finally, the mechanisms of budget execution and monitoring still favor conformity to budgetary regularity rather than the quality control of expenditure. Actions that could be taken to remedy these weaknesses include (1) devolving to the Ministry of Finance the sole responsibility for the formulation and implementation of the current and investment budgets; (2) extending the coverage of the budget law to include all treasury accounts movements; (3) breaking down all government expenditure on both a sectoral and ministerial basis; and (4) improving public expenditure monitoring and evaluation.

Finally, although Algeria's demographic trends remain overall favorable, there is a growing imbalance emerging in the social security system, resulting reportedly from difficulties in collecting social security contributions, mainly from public enterprises. The deficit was covered in 1997 by a special allocation from the supplementary budget approved in July 1997. In 1998, both social security contributions and budgetary allocations were increased. Looking ahead, the system will need to be reviewed and proposals made to ensure its long-term financial viability and thus eliminate its potential burden on the budget.

---
[7] Since 1998, the responsibility of the investment budget has been transferred to the Ministry of Finance.

V Monetary Policy and Financial Sector Reforms

Background

In the late 1980s, Algeria's financial sector was small and segmented, operating de facto as a financing instrument for public sector investment—with little linkage between risk assessment and credit allocation—while financial markets were virtually nonexistent. The five commercial banks and the savings-housing bank (Caisse nationale d'épargne et de prévoyance (CNEP))—all government-owned—had no commercial activity. They collected household and enterprise savings through an extensive network of branches, and channeled these resources to finance imports and public enterprise operations. The latter were assigned to specified banks under a policy of domiciliation. This system, under which each financial institution carried out transactions in certain sectors or dealt with specific clients, led to market segmentation, limited expertise, and lack of competition. Nonbank financial intermediaries included a few insurance companies and pension funds, also publicly owned.

The key role in the financial sector was played by the treasury, which mobilized most of the country's savings through post office savings accounts and the issue of development bonds subscribed on a compulsory basis by the insurance companies and the CNEP. These resources were used mainly for financing new projects by public enterprises, which were generally undercapitalized and relied on bank borrowing for their investments. The central bank of Algeria played a subordinate role, and interest rates were set administratively at levels that resulted in negative real interest rates, steering managers toward capital-intensive investments.

In this environment, where output targets were more important than relative prices or profitability, financial institutions played a passive role. There was neither competitive savings mobilization nor credit allocation according to risk-weighted commercial criteria. Under these conditions, the absence of market-based prudential regulations on banking was of little immediate consequence. The central bank had little supervisory activity, and its rediscount window was just an instrument to provide banks with liquidity. The rediscount system was complex, including several categories of commercial paper to which different ceilings applied, and preferential rates for credit to some sectors. Limits were mostly mandatory and preferential rates favored lending to agriculture, real estate, and major investment projects. Algeria's capital markets were virtually nonexistent, reflecting the small size of the private sector and that government bonds were nonnegotiable. Due to the presence of exchange restrictions on both current and capital account transactions, there was no integration with world financial markets.

The abundance of foreign exchange during the 1970s and early 1980s, coupled with limited reliance on market signals, allowed major imbalances in resource allocation to emerge. These misallocations resulted in low investment efficiency and an underutilization of productive capacity, as evidenced by high incremental capital output ratios. Public enterprises, operating under soft budget constraints and subject to government price and employment objectives, accumulated large debts. With mounting debt-service obligations and persisting inefficiencies, their financial situation turned precarious and, eventually, a large share of their debt became nonperforming. In 1986, with the downturn of world oil prices, the crippling effect of nonperforming assets on the balance sheet of commercial banks became apparent.

Weak financial intermediation was reflected in a ratio of currency to broad money (M2) of 40 percent and excess money balances, with a high liquidity ratio (M2/GDP) that peaked at 84 percent in 1988 (Table 7). The share of commercial bank resources accounted for by deposits was low (50 percent). As a result of the excess liquidity, parallel markets for many rationed products and for foreign exchange emerged, with prices frequently several times those on the official markets.

Financial Sector Reforms in 1989–93

In the context of Algeria's transition to a market-oriented economy, the modus operandi of the financial

V MONETARY POLICY AND FINANCIAL SECTOR REFORMS

Table 7. Monetary Survey

	\multicolumn{11}{c}{December}										
	1987	1988	1989	1990	1991	1992	1993	1994	1995	1996	1997
	\multicolumn{11}{c}{(In billions of Algerian dinars at end of period)}										
Monetary survey											
Foreign assets (net)	9.1	9.3	6.5	6.5	24.3	22.6	19.6	60.4	26.3	134.0	350.6
Net domestic assets	248.7	283.7	301.6	336.5	391.9	493.3	607.4	663.3	773.3	781.1	733.5
Domestic credit	303.7	339.2	373.0	414.0	485.7	625.1	747.6	774.4	967.2	1,057.4	1,179.7
Credit to the government (net)[1]	123.1	147.2	178.6	167.0	159.9	159.9	527.4	468.6	401.6	280.5	425.9
Credit to the economy[1]	180.6	192.0	194.4	247.0	325.8	465.2	220.2	305.8	565.6	776.8	753.8
Of which:											
Credit to 23 public enterprises	...	32.8	43.8	64.7	71.2	...	11.0	15.0	22.4	31.0	...
Credit to 12 offices2	...	...	...	...	...	...	57.7	185.9	231.0	69.1	
Other items (net)[3]	-55.1	-55.5	-71.4	-77.5	-93.8	-131.8	-140.2	-111.1	-194.0	-276.3	-411.5
Money and quasi-money (M2)	257.8	293.0	308.1	343.0	416.2	515.9	627.0	723.7	799.6	915.0	1,084.2
Money	223.8	252.2	250.0	270.1	325.9	369.7	446.5	476.0	519.1	589.1	672.8
Quasi-money	34.0	40.8	58.1	72.9	90.3	146.2	180.5	247.7	280.5	326.0	411.4
CNEP deposits	48.5	58.6	73.7	85.5	98.2	118.2	132.0	141.9	148.9	165.4	177.9
M3= M2 + CNEP deposits	306.3	351.6	381.8	428.5	514.4	634.1	759.0	865.6	948.5	1,080.4	1,262.1
Bank of Algeria											
Foreign assets (net)	9.2	6.9	3.5	2.0	12.6	17.4	17.6	50.7	15.6	122.4	343.0
Net domestic assets	93.2	104.6	122.3	136.7	149.3	180.5	234.3	186.6	239.6	183.5	13.4
Credit to the government	82.4	104.3	108.7	93.5	94.6	160.4	270.9	246.3	231.9	172.5	155.7
Credit to banks	18.2	16.9	30.7	65.7	108.4	78.3	29.4	50.4	190.3	259.1	218.9
Other items (net)[3]	-7.4	-16.7	-17.1	-22.5	-53.7	-58.3	-65.9	-110.2	-182.6	-248.0	-361.3
Reserve money	102.4	111.5	125.8	138.7	161.9	197.8	251.9	237.2	255.2	305.9	356.5
Cash in circulation	96.9	109.8	121.2	135.9	157.7	185.4	212.0	224.4	252.3	293.5	341.7
Bankers' deposits	5.5	1.7	3.8	2.0	2.5	10.9	38.4	12.9	2.9	12.4	14.9
	\multicolumn{11}{c}{(Percent change over 12-month period)}										
Money and quasi-money (M2)	13.6	13.6	5.2	11.3	21.3	23.9	21.5	15.4	10.5	14.4	18.5
Net domestic assets (banking system)	14.3	14.1	6.3	11.6	16.5	25.9	23.1	9.2	16.6	1.0	-6.1
Credit to the economy	1.6	6.3	1.3	27.0	31.9	42.8	-52.7	38.9	85.0	37.3	-3.0
Net domestic assets (central bank)	13.5	12.2	17.0	11.8	9.2	20.9	29.8	-20.4	28.4	-23.4	-92.7
Reserve money	0.0	8.9	12.3	10.3	16.7	22.2	27.4	-5.8	7.6	19.9	16.5
Liquid liabilities (M3)	15.1	14.8	8.6	12.2	20.0	23.3	19.7	14.0	9.6	13.9	16.8

(Percent change over 12-month period in terms of beginning M2 stock)

Net foreign assets	-0.1	0.1	-1.0	0.0	5.2	-0.4	-0.6	-4.7	13.5	23.7
Domestic credit	11.4	13.8	11.5	13.3	20.9	33.5	23.7	26.6	11.3	13.4
Government (net)[4]	9.7	9.3	10.7	-3.8	-2.1	0.0	71.2	-9.3	-15.1	15.9
Economy	1.6	4.4	0.8	17.1	23.0	33.5	-47.5	35.9	26.4	-2.5
Memorandum items:										
Liquidity ratio (average M2/GDP)	79.3	78.7	70.9	58.5	42.9	44.6	49.2	45.8	34.8	36.7
Liquidity ratio (end-of-period M2/GDP)	84.4	83.7	72.7	61.6	47.1	49.4	54.0	49.1	36.6	39.9
Cash in circulation/GDP	31.7	31.4	28.6	24.3	17.8	17.7	18.2	12.8	11.7	12.5
Credit to the economy/GDP[5]	59.1	54.9	45.9	44.4	36.8	44.5	19.0	20.8	31.1	26.5
Liquid liabilities (end-of-period/GDP)[6]	100.3	100.5	90.1	77.1	58.2	60.7	65.3	58.7	43.2	46.4
Velocity	1.3	1.3	1.4	1.6	2.1	2.1	2.0	2.2	2.8	2.5
GDP (in billions of Algerian dinars)	305.6	350.0	423.8	556.0	884.0	1,045.0	1,161.7	1,473.4	1,966.0	2,494.6	2,716.4
CPI (end-of-period percent change)	3.2	8.6	10.7	23.3	25.5	28.0	26.5	38.4	21.9	15.1	6.0

Sources: Bank of Algeria; and IMF staff projections.

[1]For comparison purposes, the data on credit to the government for December 1993 and December 1997 would need to be adjusted downward by DA 275.5 billion and DA 186.7 billion, respectively, representing the conversion into government bonds of public enterprises' commercial bank debt, as part of a package of financial restructuring. Data on credit to the economy need to be adjusted upward by the same amount.

[2]Includes the Société nationale des transports ferroviaires, Sonelgaz, and the 10 food-importing agencies.

[3]This includes part of the debt rescheduling proceeds that is not credited to the treasury account but instead blocked on a special account at the Bank of Algeria.

[4]This increase appears large because of the debt swap operations in 1993 (see footnote 1).

[5]This drop is due to a change in the series as explained in footnote 1. Excluding this effect, credit to the economy would represent about 40 percent of GDP in 1996.

[6]Liquid liabilities are defined to include money, quasi-money, and savings deposits at the housing bank (Caisse nationale d'épargne et de prévoyance).

V Monetary Policy and Financial Sector Reforms

sector was radically modified in 1989–91. Financial sector reforms were aimed at increasing reliance on market forces and competition, consistent with other market-oriented reforms. In response to the increasingly complex economy, the financial system had to be transformed from a mere conduit of funds from the treasury to public enterprises into a system that would play a dynamic role in resource mobilization and allocation. The key elements of such a transformation were the move to market-based instruments of monetary policy, the liberalization of interest rates, the progressive liberalization of current and capital account transactions, and the adoption of a more flexible exchange rate policy.

The first stage of reform was to establish an appropriate institutional framework. The first major step was the decision in 1987 that the treasury would withdraw from financing the economy, and from then on, would only finance investment in infrastructure and "strategic" sectors. In 1987–88, several actions were taken to increase competition: most significantly, the government abolished the requirement of allocating clients to their specific banks depending on their sectoral activity and allowed financial institutions to work in different fields. In May 1989, a money market was instituted among commercial banks, which in turn were granted autonomy from the state. The central bank intervened in this money market through the newly introduced pension mechanism, a system of repurchase agreements between commercial banks and the central bank for short-term financing.

A watershed was reached in 1990, with the passage of the law on money and credit. This law (1) granted the central bank autonomy from the Ministry of Finance to conduct monetary policy (the central bank underwent an administrative reorganization that enabled it to meet its new responsibilities and was renamed the Bank of Algeria); (2) established the Council on Money and Credit, the monetary authority responsible for formulating credit, monetary, foreign exchange, and external debt policies;[8] (3) introduced transparent rules to govern the relationship between the treasury and the financial system; and (4) established the principle of equal treatment for public and private enterprises in terms of access to credit, central bank refinancing, and interest rates, while commercial paper from the two sectors became subject to the same eligibility criteria.

Within this new institutional framework, a number of additional reforms were introduced in 1991 and 1992—a ceiling on the total access of commercial banks to central bank refinancing, while direct ceilings on commercial banks' credit to the economy were abolished, as was the case for sector-specific rediscount rates.

The Bank of Algeria introduced financial programming in 1991, but monetary policy continued to rely on four direct instruments: (1) ceilings on bank credit to enterprises and on the amount of rediscounting by banks; (2) ceilings on net bank credit to 23 large public enterprises under financial restructuring; (3) subceilings on rediscounting of bank credit to these enterprises; and (4) discretionary ceilings on Bank of Algeria interventions in the interbank money market.

A major policy shift took place in 1992. The Bank of Algeria ceased to impose credit ceilings on commercial bank lending and started relying totally on central bank refinancing of the economy. The Bank of Algeria went a step further at the end of 1993 when it started redirecting a substantial portion of commercial bank refinancing toward the money market and away from the rediscount facility. Notwithstanding these improvements, bank-by-bank ceilings on access to the rediscount window and repurchase operations imposed on each bank remained the main instruments of monetary policy.

Important steps to expand the scope of the interbank money market were taken in 1992–93. First, participation was broadened to include nonbank financial institutions (e.g., insurance companies), which were allowed to lend out their excess funds; and second, the repurchase instrument was refined to allow the Bank of Algeria greater flexibility of intervention.

Conduct of Monetary Policy Since 1994

Notwithstanding these institutional changes, Algeria's financial system was still saddled, in early 1994, by the legacy of several decades of administrative economic management. In particular, direct controls kept interest rates below market-clearing levels and limited the scope of indirect instruments of money and credit control. Moreover, the banking system, including the housing bank (CNEP), could not operate under market norms as long as many of their clients (public enterprises) were insolvent. Financial sector reforms could only succeed if public enterprise reforms were implemented at the same time. Substantial progress has been achieved on all these fronts since early 1994, when Algeria embarked on an ambitious IMF-supported program.[9]

---

[8]The council is chaired by the Governor of the Bank of Algeria, and includes the three Vice-Governors as well as three government representatives, thereby vesting the majority with the Bank of Algeria.

[9]For an overview of the rationale and the history of the reforms, and the change of orientation in the conduct of monetary policy, see Mohammed Laksaci, *Politique monétaire en Algérie* (Algiers: Bank of Algeria, March 1995).

Conduct of Monetary Policy Since 1994

Shift to Indirect Instruments of Monetary Management

By early 1994, the Bank of Algeria still controlled liquidity in the banking system by imposing ceilings on individual banks on the global amount of refinancing, and through the rediscount facility or repurchase agreements on the interbank money market. These two instruments, however, were still heavily geared to individual banks' needs and were provided at the initiative of commercial banks. As a result, it was difficult for the Bank of Algeria to control liquidity effectively, while the bank-by-bank ceilings led to severe distortions in the allocation of resources.

To address these weaknesses, starting in October 1994, the Bank of Algeria imposed a reserve requirement on commercial banks, representing 3 percent of bank deposits (excluding foreign currency deposits) and remunerated at 11.5 percent—a substantial level, considering that in some neighboring countries, reserves were not remunerated at all. The efficiency of indirect monetary control was further strengthened in May 1995 when the Bank of Algeria started repurchase auctions to provide liquidity to commercial banks.[10] These auctions aimed at increasing the role of interest rates by allowing for more competitive market practices and by providing greater transparency regarding the criteria for credit allocation.[11] Under the auction system, the Bank of Algeria announced a minimum interest rate prior to the auction; subsequently, banks bid in terms of rates and volumes. Initially, the Bank of Algeria awarded refinancing at a single interest rate (standard auction), but in late 1995, it moved to a type of Dutch auction, awarding bids at the interest rates actually offered by banks. Auctions were initially held every six weeks but, in view of their increasing importance as the main refinancing instrument, since early 1996, they have been held every three weeks. By the end of 1996, refinancing through repurchase agreements and auctions accounted for about one-half of total refinancing, compared to about one-tenth at the end of 1994.

As a further step toward deepening financial markets, the government instituted in late-1995 a formal auction system (*adjudication*) to sell negotiable treasury bonds on the money market. Interest rates on these bonds reached 22.5 percent in early 1996 before declining to 17.5 percent at the end of 1996, reflecting the slowdown in inflation. Participants in the auctions include banks and nonbank financial institutions. The system facilitated the introduction of open-market operations by the Bank of Algeria in December 1996.[12]

Interest Rate Deregulation

Commercial bank deposit rates were liberalized in May 1990, but commercial banks' lending rates still remained subject to a 20 percent ceiling a year. As a result, both types of rates remained negative in real terms in 1993–94, since they were not allowed to reflect the increasing inflationary pressures arising from the substantial relaxation of demand management policies that occurred in 1992–93. An important step taken under the 1994 reform program was, therefore, the abolition of the ceiling on commercial banks' lending rates to the public. It was accompanied by the temporary imposition of a cap of 5 percentage points on commercial bank interest rate spreads, with a view to preventing an excessive increase of lending rates as a result of possible collusion among the five commercial banks. This cap on banks' spreads was eliminated in December 1995. The deregulation of interest rates, together with the deceleration of inflation brought about by tighter demand management policies, eventually led to the emergence of positive real interest rates since the beginning of 1996 (see Table 8 and Figure 6).

The interest rates on Bank of Algeria lending to commercial banks also evolved—rediscount rates, which offered preferential treatment to certain sectors, were replaced by a uniform rate in 1992; the ceiling on money market interest rates was removed in April 1994 as well.

Foreign Exchange Management

Several measures where taken in 1989–91 to liberalize the trade and exchange regimes (see Section VII). This initial set of reforms turned out to be insufficient, and in the face of a sharp deterioration of Algeria's external situation from 1992 onward, the authorities intensified trade and exchange controls. The reform program initiated in April 1994 included trade and payments liberalization combined with a large depreciation of the Algerian dinar. Fixing sessions for foreign exchange at the Bank of Algeria were

---

[10]The Bank of Algeria maintained the rediscount window in parallel with the auction system for a transition period to ensure that the liquidity needs of commercial banks were met.

[11]The introduction of the auction mechanism followed a number of actions taken in 1994 aimed at strengthening both banking institutions and public enterprises. Public enterprises acquired management and financial autonomy; nonperforming loans were transferred to the state in exchange for treasury bonds; and performance contracts were introduced to impose discipline and efficiency norms on public enterprise managers. At the level of commercial banks, credit risks were addressed through an ongoing bank recapitalization program and the restructuring of the 23 largest loss-making public enterprises, including their debt.

[12]For a discussion of the rationale for the introduction of new monetary instruments in Algeria, see Karim Djoudi, *Marché monétaire et innovations financières* (Algiers: Bank of Algeria, April 1995).

V MONETARY POLICY AND FINANCIAL SECTOR REFORMS

Table 8. Structure of Interest Rates
(In percent per year)

	Oct. 1991–Apr. 1994	Effective Apr. 12, 1994	As of Dec. 1994	As of Dec. 1995	As of Dec. 1996	As of Dec. 1997
Central bank rediscount	11.50	15.00	15.00	14.00	13.00	11.00
Central bank overdraft	20.00	24.00	24.00	24.00	24.00	24.00
Money market						
Repurchase agreements[1,2]	17.00	20.00	21.00–22.00	23.00	19.00–21.00	13.33
Auctions	...	...	...	19.50	17.20	14.50
Commercial banks' deposit rate[3,4]	12.00–16.00	16.50–18.00	16.50–18.00	16.50–18.00	16.50–18.00	8.50–12.00
Commercial banks' lending rate[5]	15.00–20.00	18.00–25.00	18.00–25.00	19.00–24.00	17.00–21.50	9.00–13.00
Foreign currency deposits denominated in U.S. dollars[6]	4.00	6.00	6.73	5.75	5.70	5.74
Caisse nationale d'épargne et de prévoyance (savings and housing)						
Deposit rate						
Savings	8.00	14.00	14.00	16.00	16.00	16.00
Housing	5.00	10.00	10.00	12.00	12.00	12.00
Lending rate (housing)						
Individuals[7]	7.00–14.00	11.60–15.00	12.00–22.00	12.00–22.00	12.00–22.00	10.30–17.50
Developers	14.00	15.00–19.00	16.00–20.00	16.00–20.00	16.00–20.00	10.00–17.50
Treasury bonds						
Negotiable						
13 weeks	...	...	...	...	...	12.93
26 weeks	...	...	...	...	...	13.93
Non negotiable						
12 months	10.00	10.00	10.00	10.00	10.00	10.00
24 months	11.25	11.25	11.25	11.25	11.25	11.25
36 months	13.00	13.00	13.00	13.00	13.00	13.00
Equipment bonds						
1 year	9.50	16.50	16.50	...	...	...
2 years	10.25	...	...	...	...	...
3–20 years	11.00–15.00	11.00–15.00	11.00–15.00	11.00–15.00	11.00–15.00	11.00–15.00

Sources: Algerian authorities, central bank of Algeria, and Ministry of Finance.
[1]Central bank overnight rate.
[2]The ceiling on money market rates (18 percent) was abolished in April 1994.
[3]In May 1990, deposit rates were liberalized, but remained in pratice constrained by ceilings on lending rates.
[4]No interest is paid on sight deposits; interest on term deposits is subject to a 15 percent securities revenue tax, whereas government bond yields are tax exempt.
[5]Prior to May 1990, lending rates were not allowed to exceed 3 percentage points above banks' average cost of resources; starting from that date, they were subject to a ceiling of 20 percent a year. This ceiling was removed in April 1994, but a maximum margin of five points was imposed on banks until December 1995.
[6]Free for banks to determine on the basis of LIBOR plus 150 basis points.
[7]Based on the average cost of resources plus five percentage points.

superseded by the establishment of an interbank foreign exchange market in December 1995. In December 1996, the Bank of Algeria authorized the establishment of foreign exchange bureaus. These institutional changes have greatly enhanced the Bank of Algeria's capacity to manage monetary policy, increasing effective control of liquidity, and have enhanced transparency and efficiency in credit allocation with the increased reliance on market and price mechanisms and the shift away from direct controls. These changes have also complemented and supported recent reforms in other sectors, improving resource allocation and paving the way for the introduction of current account convertibility at the end of 1997.

Monetary Developments Since 1991

Monetary developments since 1991 can be decomposed into two contrasting periods that reflect a dramatic change in the macroeconomic stance. During 1992–93, monetary policy was essentially expansion-

Monetary Developments Since 1991

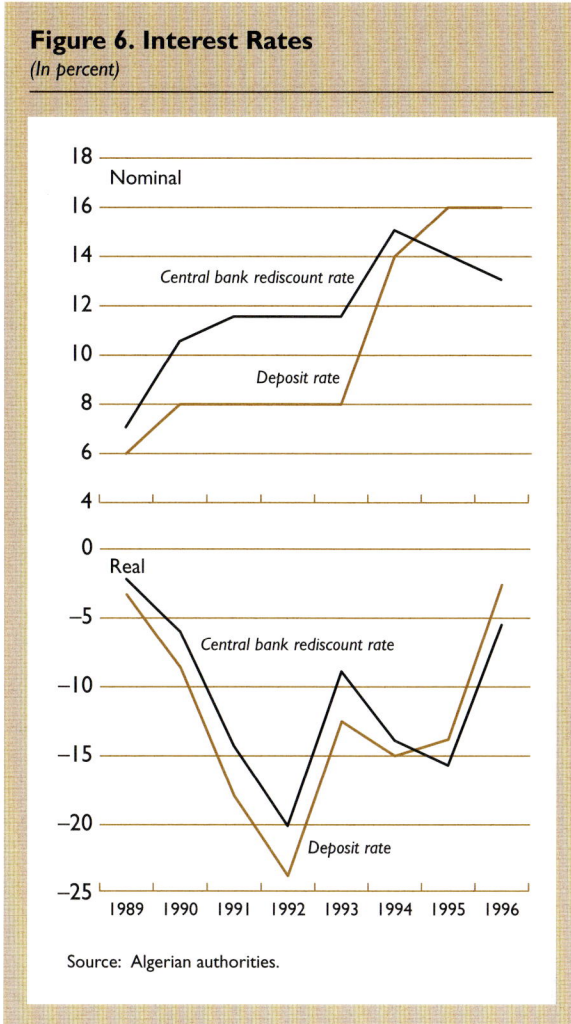

Figure 6. Interest Rates
(In percent)

Source: Algerian authorities.

ary, geared to financing large budget deficits and credit needs of public enterprises. Moreover, a sizable share of the increase in bank credit during the period could be ascribed to the needs of the Rehabilitation Fund, established to finance public enterprise restructuring. By contrast, starting in 1994, monetary policy was tightened significantly with the aim of reducing inflation and supporting exchange rate stability.

During 1992–93, as a result of the lack of fiscal discipline and concomitant monetary loosening, the stock of total outstanding credit to government almost trebled (Table 7). At the same time, credit to the economy increased markedly in response to high demand from enterprises, whose financial situation had deteriorated owing to large wage increases and a general slowdown in the economy. In addition, banks had no choice but to extend credit to enterprises to enable them to meet their external debt obligations.

Consequently, broad money increased annually by 22 percent over 1992–93, largely reflecting domestic credit expansion—international reserves were stable over the period and thus played a limited role. Fiscal expansion and wage increases, coupled with shortages owing to import compression, led to excess liquidity and a monetary overhang, as reflected by an increase in the liquidity ratio by more than 4 percentage points from the end of 1991 to the end of 1993. During 1991–93, however, inflation actually declined, from 25.5 percent in the 12 months to December 1991 to about 20.5 percent on average for 1993. But the consumer price index did not reflect underlying inflation, particularly in 1993, because of the imposition of price controls and the emergence of shortages, which led in turn to the emergence of black markets and a large premium between the official and the parallel exchange rate. By contrast, the extensive price adjustments and liberalization and the Algerian dinar depreciations that took place in 1994 led to a sharp temporary increase of the CPI that year, to a peak of 38.4 percent by the end of December 1994, which was accompanied by a rapid increase in velocity (Figure 7). The marked decline in the share of currency in M2 during the period is noteworthy, as households attempted to protect the value of their savings against inflation (see Box 5).

Starting in 1994, in the context of the reform program, monetary policy was tightened to achieve a rapid reduction in inflation. This policy was supported by the dramatic turnaround in the fiscal position, with a reduction in the budget deficit by more than 4 percentage points of GDP in 1994 and 3 percentage points of GDP in 1995. Fiscal restraint and the emergence of surpluses contributed to the steady decline in the stock of outstanding credit to government, which by the end of 1996 stood at about one-half of the December 1991 level. Credit to the rest of the economy plummeted in 1994, but gradually increased thereafter, along with the recovery in economic activity. In support of macroeconomic adjustment, the external debt relief granted in 1994 and 1995—as well as more favorable world oil prices in 1996 and 1997—allowed for an impressive strengthening of Algeria's external position. Indeed, international reserves rose from $1.5 billion by the end of 1993 to $8.0 billion by the end of 1997.

Accordingly, broad money expansion slowed down in 1994–97. The excess liquidity created during the previous period was rapidly absorbed, and the liquidity ratio (M2/GDP) declined from 49 percent in December 1993 to below 37 percent in December 1997. The tighter monetary conditions resulted in a substantial reduction in inflation, from 39 percent in 1994 to 21 percent in 1995 and 15 percent in 1996, and below 6 percent by the end of 1997—a remarkable performance, particularly in light of the 50 percent devaluation that took place at the outset of the program period. That a substantial output recovery could

V MONETARY POLICY AND FINANCIAL SECTOR REFORMS

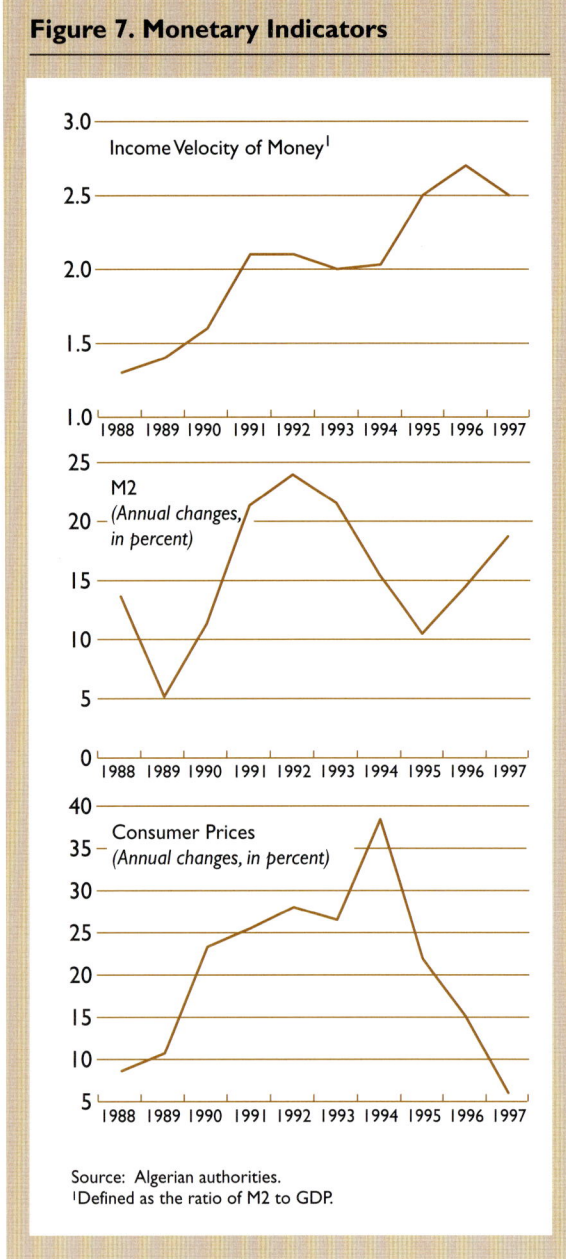

Figure 7. Monetary Indicators

Source: Algerian authorities.
[1]Defined as the ratio of M2 to GDP.

Commercial Bank Restructuring Efforts

Before the reforms, Algerian commercial banks lacked the institutional framework and the experience to promote efficient financial intermediation. They were burdened by a legacy of compulsory lending to public enterprises, sectoral credit specialization, and inadequate prudential regulations, which weakened the quality of their portfolios considerably. The solvency of the banking sector deteriorated greatly over the years, to the extent that, by 1990, 65 percent of banks' assets were nonperforming, and recourse to central bank refinancing was increasing at an alarming rate. To address these problems, a major financial reform package was adopted in May 1991 to restructure the banking and public enterprise sectors. This reform was supported financially and technically by the World Bank's Enterprise and Financial Sector Adjustment Loan, which recognized the close financial interlinkages between banks and public enterprises. Under this reform package, in 1992–93, the government took over DA 275 billion of nonperforming banks' claims on public enterprises (equivalent to 60 percent of the outstanding bank credit to the economy and 23 percent of 1992 GDP)[14] in exchange for government bonds bearing annual interest rates of 10 percent with 12 years' maturity.[15]

Starting in 1994, efforts were aimed at ensuring that commercial banks conformed to upgraded standards for banking operations and accounting and initiated a program of internal and financial restructuring. All existing banks were required to reapply for certification with the Bank of Algeria, which, as noted earlier, started imposing reserve requirements in October 1994. Subsequently, the authorities conducted audits, in collaboration with the World Bank, to determine the banks' recapitalization needs to meet a minimum capital/risk-weighted assets ratio of 5 percent in 1996. This is to be increased to 8 percent by 1999, in line with Bank of International Settlements standards.[16] At the end of 1994, audits of balance sheets had been completed for four of Algeria's five commercial banks, indicating that,

materialize over 1995–97—despite the significant tightening of monetary conditions—bears witness to the fact that, under the new monetary policy, it was possible to channel credit efficiently toward more productive activities.[13]

---

[13]Mohammed Laksaci in *Une conjoncture financière et monétaire favorable à la reprise* (Algiers: Bank of Algeria, April 1995) underscores that an efficient credit allocation becomes all the more important if the ambitious growth objectives are to materialize, while monetary policy must continue to be geared toward achieving the convergence of Algeria's inflation rate to the level prevalent in its partner countries.

[14]These ratios are for illustrative purposes only, since a stock of nonperforming loans accumulated over several years are compared to one year's output.

[15]The amount was assessed on the basis of the financial restructuring of the 23 loss-making enterprises and audits of the five commercial banks at the end of 1991, and involved the issuance of nonnegotiable government bond to the banks. About 70 percent of these bonds were subsequently redeemed between 1992 and 1995.

[16]B. Achari in *Typologie des risques bancaires et réglementation prudentielle* (Algiers: Bank of Algeria, 1995) provides an overview of the main measures undertaken by the Bank of Algeria since 1994 to improve banking supervision and strengthen the financial position of commercial banks in Algeria.

Box 5. Determinants of Inflation

In the 20 years up to 1990, when price liberalization started, annual inflation in Algeria averaged about 9 percent. Inflation only surged once, after the first oil shock in the early 1970s, reflecting higher import prices and strong demand pressures in the nontradables sector owing to the oil windfall. But price stability was only apparent: large budget deficits were being monetized, causing a monetary overhang, and inflationary pressures were repressed by pervasive price controls—in 1990, more than 50 percent of the items in the consumer price index (CPI) were subject to either price ceilings or margin limits—which resulted in widespread supply shortages. In the early 1990s, large devaluations led to increasing inflation, but also growing import and external debt-servicing costs, leading to higher budget deficits and mounting public enterprise losses. These imbalances were financed through money creation and, by the end of 1992, the 12-month inflation rate was 28 percent.

The 1994 stabilization program included a large up-front devaluation geared to improving competitiveness and restoring external viability over the medium term. The devaluation contributed to an initial increase in inflation, which reached 39 percent at the end of 1994, but a restrictive fiscal policy, a tight incomes policy and a nonaccommodating monetary stance soon led to sharp declines. By the end of 1996, the 12-month rate of inflation was down to 15 percent, and to 7 percent by the end of March 1997. This performance was all the more remarkable in the midst of price liberalization: administered prices more than doubled over 1994–96, and by early 1996, only less than 15 percent of the items in the CPI were regulated. While price liberalization allowed for the realignment of relative prices, its inflationary impact was minimized by a prudent monetary stance, which made room for those adjustments without feeding inflationary pressures. The recovery in money demand,

Share in the CPI of Regulated Prices

	1990	May 1991	October 1991	April 1995
Share in CPI (in percent)	52.7	38.8	28.2	15.2

in the wake of the successful stabilization effort, also contributed to the favorable inflation outcome.

The government's public sector wage policy was instrumental in reducing inflation. Wages declined in real terms by more than 30 percent over 1993–96, which helped to restore competitiveness. Wages were adjusted not on the basis of past inflation, but taking into consideration inflation expectations based on external prospects and productivity gains and, in the event, wage awards were consistently below inflation. The absence of widespread indexation mechanisms also contributed greatly to curb inflationary inertia. Furthermore, in early 1997, a two-year agreement for moderate wage increases in the civil service was reached, while wage increases in public enterprises were effectively delinked from civil service wage increases, and are to be based on the financial situation of each enterprise.

A simple econometrics exercise using ordinary least squares (OLS) attempts to identify some of the determinants of inflation in Algeria. From the second quarter of 1988 to the fourth quarter of 1996, three variables were found to be significant and influence price developments: changes in the money supply (M2), the nominal effective exchange rate, and movements in world oil prices.

Some Determinants of Inflation
(t-ratios in parentheses)

Dependent Variable	M2 Expansion	Changes in Nominal Effective Exchange Rate	Changes in World Oil Prices	
Inflation (CPI end of period)	1.035 (7.53)	0.1375 (2.37)	0.07 (2.33)	R2 = 0.43 DW = 2.0

V MONETARY POLICY AND FINANCIAL SECTOR REFORMS

of the five state-owned banks, only the Banque Nationale d'Algérie did not need additional capital. On the basis of audits for 1995 and more recent supervision data collected by the Bank of Algeria, some additional recapitalization needs were identified for three public banks in 1998.[17]

Over 1991–96, commercial banks received DA 217 billion in cash, of which about 80 percent compensated for foreign exchange losses incurred on past external borrowing contracted on behalf of the state, while the remaining 20 percent went almost entirely for banks' recapitalization. The Banque Extérieure d'Algérie and the Crédit Populaire d'Algérie were recapitalized in 1995 through budgetary contributions of DA 10 billion. The recapitalization has been financed by additional government interventions:

- first, in 1996, the government issued DA 24.9 billion of 20-year bonds to recapitalize four of the five public commercial banks (excluding the Banque Extérieure d'Algérie);

- second, during April 1997, DA 8 billion were disbursed by the budget to recapitalize the CNEP upon its transformation into a housing bank;

- third, during the first quarter of 1997, the government swapped DA 187 billion of nonperforming bank loans for 12-year treasury bonds (also in exchange for the nonperforming loans of the Société nationale des transports ferroviaires, Sonelgaz, and food- and pharmaceutical-importing agencies). This operation amounted to 24 percent of the stock of commercial bank credit to the economy at the end of 1996, and led to an increase in interest payments in the 1997 budget of about 0.6 percent of GDP.

The recapitalization of each bank was accompanied by the signing of performance contracts between the government and bank managers. Performance contracts hold the bank managers directly and solely responsible for respecting the capital adequacy ratios established by the Bank of Algeria. The banks, in turn, are being provided with increased autonomy with respect to operational decisions, notably the allocation of credit and, mainly,

the denial of credit to high-risk enterprises.[18] In this context, commercial banks started in 1996 to reschedule some of the debt of certain public enterprises by converting short-term overdrafts into medium-term loans. These debt restructuring operations have been conditioned upon the liquidation of a number of nonviable units within otherwise viable enterprises, the implementation of performance contracts by public enterprise managers, and equity participation from commercial banks (see Box 6).

In addition, in early 1995, the Bank of Algeria started to implement new prudential regulations that limit risk concentration and establish clear rules for loan classification and provisioning. In particular, banks are now required (1) to limit overdrafts to the equivalent of 15 days' turnover (compared with 45 days previously); (2) not to register overdue interest payments as revenues; and (3) to establish provisions for off-balance sheet claims. This new framework is expected to tighten the budget constraint on banks and increase the incentives for bank managers to mobilize financial savings, improve the allocation of credit, and search for potential private partners.

Several measures were also taken to promote competition in the banking sector. An amendment to the Investment Code was introduced in 1994 to allow foreign participation in the capital of domestic banks and, although the five major commercial banks remain government-owned, the government is actively seeking a buyer for the Banque de Développement Local (the existing 49 percent limit to private ownership does not apply if a foreign investor is buying a bank in its entirety). Furthermore, a new private bank was chartered in September 1995 (Union Bank), along with the Caisse nationale de mutualité agricole, owned by private agricultural cooperatives. More private banks were authorized in 1997, including Citibank and Arab Bank.

Agenda for Further Reforms

Substantial progress has been made in the last few years in addressing the problems of the financial sector: establishing a sound and market-based system of bank intermediation; moving toward the use of indirect and market-based instruments for the conduct of monetary policy; and ensuring the use of market-based mechanisms for the mobilization of

---

[17]The audit is being completed for the Banque Algérienne de Développement Rural, whose financial situation has suffered from large nonperforming loans mainly to food-importing agencies. This problem was tackled in early 1997 through the takeover of these loans by the government in exchange for government bonds, for an amount of DA 187 billion (of which DA 50 billion for the debts of the Société nationale de l'électricité (Sonelgaz) and the Société nationale des transports ferroviaires, and the remainder for the debt of food- and pharmaceutical-importing agencies). The restructuring and financing needs of the CNEP are discussed in Chapter VI.

[18]This was dramatically demonstrated at the end of 1995, when banks denied credit to several loss-making public enterprises (mostly in construction), resulting in layoffs of 130,000 workers and a general strike in February 1996.

Box 6. Bank-Enterprises Mechanism

• Prereform financial practices resulted in the accumulation of a massive amount of nonperforming loans by the banking sector. The adjustment and liberalization process exacerbated the problem, as inefficient state enterprises, unable to withstand competition and their external debt-service costs, which had more than doubled owing to the Algerian dinar devaluation, saw their financial position deteriorate further. To address the problem, banks were progressively recapitalized and public enterprises received large transfers from the treasury transfers mainly through the Rehabilitation Fund created in 1991. These partial measures, however, did not suffice. Public enterprises continued to lose market share while their low productivity impaired their ability to meet future financial obligations and to make adequate use of new financial resources. In view of the rapidly mounting restructuring costs, the Algerian authorities embarked on a new strategy that would move away from financial transfers from the budget and be geared toward protecting the strength of the financial sector and restoring the medium-term profitability of public enterprises in a market-driven economy. As part of the new strategy, the bank-enterprises mechanism was set up in September 1996, while the Rehabilitation Fund ceased operations at the end of 1996.

• The bank-enterprises mechanism's immediate objective was to address the mounting overdrafts at high interest rates of public enterprises and then restore progressively their financial situation. After a comprehensive audit of the enterprises' accounts, the commercial banks and the 11 holdings that now group all large public enterprises, together with representatives from the central bank and the treasury, identified viable and nonviable production units. A plan was set up to normalize the financial relationship between economically viable enterprises and the banking system, with a large share of the overdrafts consolidated into medium-term loans at lower interest rates. The amount to be consolidated was estimated at DA 89.8 billion, equivalent to 14.1 percent of the end-March 1997 stock of total credit to the economy (excluding the 12 food-importing agencies and the utilities company and the railways). At the same time, stringent programs were adopted to compel enterprises to increase their productivity and to provide them with financial autonomy. Accordingly, the plan included the establishment of more than 502 subsidiary units with competitive prospects operating under tight bank supervision by the end of 1998 (of which 307 were in place by the end of December 1997). The operation was viewed by the authorities as a first step toward their privatization, expected to take place before the end of 1998.

• Nonviable enterprises are being liquidated: from the end of November 1996 to the end of September 1997, 76 enterprises and 64 production units were liquidated. The reduction of excess labor in public enterprises is expected to lead to an increase in productivity. As of the end of December 1997, 158,936 employees had been laid off (see table below).

Impact on Holdings of Bank-Enterprises Agreements Through December 1997
(Excluding local enterprises)

Holdings	Situation Before End-November 1996		Situation at End-December 1997		Gross Employment Reduction
	Number of enterprises	Number of employees	Enterprises liquidated	Remaining employees	
Food processing	13	32,098	4	13,973	13,782
Agro-industry	12	47,226	1	42,972	8,873
Services	102	65,001	23	63,541	15,523
Mechanical industry	17	41,706	2	31,321	14,491
Construction	119	124,935	23	102,810	35,767
Manufacturing	24	69,569	1	48,582	23,056
Electricity and telecommunications	20	33,028	5	22,866	12,041
Mining	7	10,736	1	10,423	395
Pharmaceuticals, chemicals	19	34,617	4	30,639	8,239
Public works	66	74,040	12	66,700	13,466
Steel industry	12	46,985	0	42,632	13,323
Total	411	579,941	76	476,459	158,936

Source: Algerian authorities.

V MONETARY POLICY AND FINANCIAL SECTOR REFORMS

Box 7. Monetary Control and Financial Reforms

In the context of Algeria's transition to a market-based economy, the modus operandi of the financial sector has been radically modified during the last years. From a mono-bank-type system, where the treasury played a direct role in financing the economy by directing credit through state-owned commercial banks to inefficient, loss-making public enterprises, Algeria is moving progressively toward a modern market-based financial system.

Monetary regulation. In the late 1980s, a first round of measures was taken to improve the functioning of the banking sector, including the creation of a money market among commercial banks. The latter were granted autonomy from the state, and the system of repurchase agreements between commercial banks and the Central Bank of Algeria for short-term financing was introduced. In 1990, the Law on Money and Credit established a new monetary framework, which made some headway toward laying the institutional foundation of an independent central bank. In 1992, the Central Bank of Algeria ceased to impose credit ceilings on commercial bank lending and started relying totally on central bank refinancing of the economy. In October 1994, the Central Bank of Algeria imposed a remunerated reserve requirement on commercial banks (at 3 percent of deposits, excluding foreign currency deposits). Repurchase auctions to provide liquidity to commercial banks were introduced in May 1995. These aimed at increasing the role of interest rates by allowing competitive market practices to prevail and by ensuring greater transparency regarding the criteria for credit allocation. The number of auctions has increased steadily and they are now held every three weeks. Finally, open market operations were formally introduced at the end of 1996, although activity remains low because of excess liquidity currently present in the banking system and the limited supply of tradeable securities available to deepen the market. As regards interest rates, they were progressively liberalized during this process. Ceilings on lending rates were replaced by controls on interest rate spreads, then all controls were removed. Positive real interest rates emerged in early 1996.

Foreign exchange management. Fixing sessions for foreign exchange at the Central Bank of Algeria were superseded by the establishment of an interbank foreign exchange market in December 1995. To improve access to foreign exchange, the Central Bank of Algeria authorized the establishment of *bureaux de change* in December 1996. These have proliferated in 1997.

Bank restructuring/the regulatory framework. To strengthen financial intermediation in the economy, a major effort has been made to revamp the banking sector. In 1992–93, the government took over DA 275 billion of the banks' nonperforming claims on public enterprises (equivalent to 60 percent of outstanding bank credit to the economy and 23 percent of 1992 GDP) in exchange for government bonds. The Rehabilitation Fund was closed at the end of 1996; the last disbursement (DA 10 billion) took place in December 1997, ending the recapitalization of banks. Since 1995, new prudential norms have been implemented, including limits on the concentration of risk and clear rules for loan classification and provisioning. At present, banks have to meet a capital/risk weighted asset ratio of 4 percent, which will increase to the BIS norm of 8 percent by 1999. To ensure that banks are complying with the new requirements, all banks will need to be relicensed by the Central Bank of Algeria. Two have already been relicensed, including a newly created private bank. To complete this process, bank audits are under way and are expected to be finalized by the end of 1997. Financial discipline imposed by banks in state enterprises has led to an improvement of bank loan portfolios. Moreover, to improve the operation of the banking system and to protect depositors, a limited deposit guarantee mechanism was introduced in December 1997. Finally, a program to modernize the payments system, aimed in particular at expediting intra- and interbank transactions, will be carried out with the technical support of the World Bank.

Broadening of financing instruments. To increase the number and type of financial instruments available, a stock market is expected to be operational before the end of 1997. The Commission for Stock Market Organization and Supervision has been created, as well as the Securities Exchange Management company. In this regard, Algeria has benefited from technical assistance provided by Canada, France, and Tunisia for personnel training. The first bond quotations should appear in December 1997, and stocks are expected to trade on the market in February 1998.

Housing finance. The housing bank (CNEP) was transformed into a mortgage bank, operating on a commercial basis in April 1997. A mortgage refinancing company and a mortgage guarantee company were created in September and December 1997, respectively. These two companies should help to broaden the financing possibilities for housing, including by enticing other financial institutions into the market.

---

domestic financing for the budget (see Box 7). Indeed, indicators reveal that the volume and efficiency of financial intermediation grew considerably in the course of the reforms.[19] Nonetheless, further reforms are still required to boost financial savings and promote an efficient allocation of resources.

---

[19]See Abdelali Jbili, Klaus Enders, and Volker Treichel, *Financial Sector Reforms in Algeria, Morocco, and Tunisia: A Preliminary Assessment* (Washington: International Monetary Fund, 1997). In their study, econometric analysis provided some evidence that, on the one hand, financial sector reform did strengthen savings in Algeria. On the other hand, consistent with other studies, direct effects of financial sector reforms on growth were more difficult to pinpoint.

First, high in the reform agenda is the deepening of the secondary market for government paper. Such a deepening would establish yield curves that would act as a benchmark to help guide intertemporal decisions and facilitate the conduct of open-market operations by the Bank of Algeria.

Second, efforts at strengthening the financial position of existing banks will have to continue so that they can achieve their targeted capital adequacy ratios and become profitable, which would facilitate their privatization. In this connection, steps will have to be taken to prevent the recurrence of large-scale nonperforming loans to public enterprises: on the one hand, success in banking reform will depend crucially on the consolidation of the public enterprise sector and the Bank of Algeria's continued monitoring of commercial banks. On the other hand, competition among banks will need to be fostered, by the development of nonbank (stock and bond) financial markets. In this regard, further liberalization of entry into the sector, as well as privatization and increased foreign participation, would add dynamism to the sector by encouraging the adoption of new management practices and the acquisition of foreign expertise. The process of liberalization and deepening of domestic financial markets should eventually culminate with the liberalization of capital movements and a move to full convertibility that would expose domestic financial markets further to competition from world markets.

Third, steps will have to be taken to broaden the availability of long-term financing, by fostering the development of markets for commercial paper, mortgages, and other long-term instruments. In this respect, high priority must be given to completing CNEP restructuring, which is under way (see Section VI).

Finally, a stock market is being established. As a first step, a Commission for Stock Market Organization and Supervision was established in early 1997. Functioning equity markets are essential to promote a modern private sector, since they mobilize savings and constitute an alternative source of equity financing for enterprises as they help overcome the constraints of family-based traditional enterprises. They may also become a major instrument in mobilizing domestic and foreign savings to finance privatization—as illustrated by Egypt's and Morocco's successful experiences—and would be a key element for the success of privatization operations.

VI The Social Dimension of Adjustment

Issues of income distribution, unemployment, housing, and social welfare have always loomed large in Algeria. With a young and rapidly growing population, the labor force has been increasing faster than job opportunities. The consequent unemployment, coupled with rapid urbanization and an existing housing shortage, has placed a severe strain on the social fabric and the provision of basic social services. Nevertheless, Algeria entered the 1990s with less acute poverty and inequalities in income distribution than other countries in the region with similar income levels.

The 1994 reform program had important implications in this regard. Prior to the reform, the government had tried to provide a social safety net via generalized subsidies, extensive and sheltered employment in the public sector, and income transfers. This system was both inequitable and inefficient, and, with growing fiscal imbalances, it also became financially unsustainable. Measures that had to be undertaken to liberalize the economy—trade and price liberalization, public sector enterprise restructuring and privatization, financial sector reform, and the overhaul of the housing delivery system—as well as the sharp decline in real wages entailed by the adjustment process, shook the existing paradigm of social protection and rendered its transformation unavoidable.

It was clear that an improvement in living conditions was essential to gain the support of the population for the reform program, especially in a difficult political and social environment. Therefore, the program included measures aimed at mitigating the transitional costs of structural adjustment for the most vulnerable sectors of the population, mainly through the overhaul of the social safety net, including the replacement of the previous system of low and poorly targeted income transfers by a self-targeted public works program, and the establishment of an unemployment insurance scheme.

Ultimately, the success of reforms will be measured by the ability of the Algerian economy to bring about a sustained improvement in the welfare of the population. Thus, over the medium term, a key challenge for Algeria will be its ability to provide adequate education, health, infrastructure, and housing services; to create sufficient employment opportunities to reduce the existing unemployment and absorb new entrants; and to protect the most vulnerable sectors of the population. This section seeks to identify the main problems underlying these challenges and reviews the strategies that are being pursued to address them.

Unemployment

Algeria's population in 1995 was estimated at 29.6 million, of which more than one-half were under the age of 20. While population growth has been steadily slowing in the recent decade, to an estimated 2.1 percent in 1995, the higher rates in the 1970s and 1980s explain the young age structure of the population. As a result of this age structure, the labor force has been growing much faster than the population, at a rate of nearly 4 percent a year in 1981–95.[20] Total labor force, however, stood at an estimated 7.1 million in 1995, only 25 percent of the population, owing to the large school enrollment and low participation of women compared with other countries in the region. Nevertheless, labor force participation has been rising in recent years.[21] In particular, the marked increase in the female participation rate—despite increased schooling, which led to declining participation rates for younger women—may indicate a response to falling real wages and large family size.

Since the pace of employment creation in the past decade was insufficient to absorb the large number of new entrants in the labor force, unemployment escalated from 10 percent in 1985 to 25 percent in 1995, when an estimated 5.3 million Algerians were

---

[20]Reflecting an ongoing exodus from rural areas into cities, the urban population has been growing even faster, at 4.8 percent on average during 1981–90, and only in recent years did its growth fall below 4 percent (Office National des Statistiques, *Retrospective 1962–1991*, No. 35, Algiers, 1991).

[21]The participation rate rose from 36 percent of all persons 15 years to 64 years of age in 1977 to 41 percent in 1991 on account of both rising male (from 71 percent to 75 percent) and female participation rates (from 3.5 percent to 6.7 percent).

employed, and 1.8 million unemployed.[22] Thus, on average, the earnings of one employed person was needed to support five people. Among the employed, self-employment remains substantial, probably a reflection of a large service sector and the importance of agriculture. The structure of unemployment also remains quite skewed (see Box 8).

Dynamics of Unemployment

Labor market prospects remain extremely clouded, a matter of great concern to Algerian policymakers.[23] With the tightening of further migration to western Europe, the future evolution of labor supply in Algeria will be mainly determined by two elements: (1) the evolution of the population aged 15 and over and (2) the likely evolution of the labor force participation rate. Regarding the latter, one would expect male labor force participation to accelerate as the fraction of men aged 12 to 25 years and attending school is reduced; female labor force participation is also likely to continue to rise, as an increasing proportion of women will take advantage of their education to join the labor market and raise household income. Under the assumption that participation (as a percentage of the population) continues to rise through 2010 in line with recent trends, while population growth continues to slow down, about 250,000 people would be added on a net basis to the Algerian labor market annually.

Appendix II presents some unemployment projections under a "low-growth" scenario and a "high-growth" scenario. Under the low-growth scenario, and assuming high elasticities of employment/output creation, unemployment would fall to 26 percent by 2001 and 24 percent by 2010. Making more pessimistic assumptions on elasticities, unemployment would rise rapidly to about 31 percent by 2001 and 37 percent by 2010. Under the high-growth scenario, and assuming high elasticities, unemployment would fall to 23 percent by 2001 and be reduced to about 8 percent by 2010. Assuming low elasticities, high growth would be insufficient to reduce unemployment, which would gradually rise to 32 percent by 2010. These projections underscore the need for growth to be not only high and sustainable, but also more labor-intensive than in the past.

---

[22]A labor survey conducted in 1996 estimated unemployment at 28 percent. Current measures may overstate Algeria's unemployment rate, however, since the definition used is wider than the International Labor Organization's definition, that is, underemployed individuals can classify themselves as unemployed in the reference week. (S. Al-Qudsi, R. Assaad, and R. Shaban, "Labor Markets in Arab Countries: A Survey," presented at the First Annual Conference on Development Economics, Cairo, 1993).

[23]For an analysis of labor markets in Algeria, see Klaus Enders, "Labor Market Prospects in Algeria" (unpublished mimeo: International Monetary Fund, 1996).

Reasons for Unemployment

Several explanations may be advanced to account for the high level of unemployment. First, the growth rate of real non-oil GDP between 1985–95 has been substantially below the rate of increase of the labor force and the increase in the labor participation rate. Second, major distortions in the price system and an overvaluation of the exchange rate that prevailed until 1994 favored capital-intensive technology. Third, the adjustment process has resulted in some labor shedding, whereas the participation rate has increased, particularly among women. Fourth, there are distortions embodied in certain features of the institutional structure of the Algerian labor market and labor regulations that may have reduced employment in the formal sector while raising it in the informal sector. Finally, educational and geographical mismatches also play an important role.

- Insufficient job creation in private sector. About 1 million job seekers entered the market during 1991–95, while the economy created only 0.4 million new jobs—virtually all in the public sector (0.1 million) and in commerce and services (0.3 million); employment in agriculture, industry, and construction broadly stagnated. Similar trends had been observed during 1985–91. Important differences were also observable in private and public sector hiring: annual growth rates of employment during 1985–89 in privately owned industrial and construction firms averaged 6 percent and 10 percent, respectively, albeit from a small base. These trends are likely to have accelerated since.

- Trade unions, minimum wages, and wage bargaining. The legally binding minimum wage (*salaire national minimum garanti*, SNMG) is set by the "*tripartite*"—the government in consultation with labor unions (the Union Générale des Travailleurs Algériens, which until 1990 had a statutory monopoly) and employers (both public and private) at the national level. Additional agreements (*conventions collectives*) are struck at the sectoral level, within the limits set out by national settlements. Civil service salaries are determined according to a grid that, in the past, was also valid for public enterprises. Following the introduction of the new labor code in 1990, public enterprises were granted more autonomy in wage setting. Civil service salaries, however, still served as a reference point. In the past, both increases in the minimum wage and the average wage were negotiated for the public sector. For instance, in 1994, the agreed salary increase applied to all public enterprises, even those that were shedding labor under restructuring plans, and where workers had accepted to trade salary

VI THE SOCIAL DIMENSION OF ADJUSTMENT

increases against job retention. This policy caused major financial problems for some enterprises and, in 1996, the policy was abandoned. Thereafter, only increases in the minimum wage are decided at the national level.

- Evolution of wages. The institutional setup of the labor market has likely contributed to upward pressures on wages. Data on minimum wages and public sector wages provide some indication of union pressures. The minimum wage rose in real terms by about 17 percent during 1989–93, while total labor productivity fell by 12 percent; the real minimum wage subsequently fell sharply during 1994–97, while productivity increased. Indicators of compensation levels in the private sector suggest that wages for the unskilled are substantially higher than the SNMG. In addition, the bias against labor—through the subsidization of capital[24]—in the 1980s was tackled by the sharp Algerian dinar devaluation and the increase in interest rates to positive real levels following the 1994 reform. Government wages also have been falling in real terms since 1993, and by 10 percent during 1995 alone. While remaining well above the SNMG, a more compressed wage distribution is emerging in the public sector. Wage levels in the private sector are thought to be lower for low-skill jobs, but more dispersed at higher-skill levels. The much larger share of the wage bill in total output observed in the public sector, compared to the private sector, suggests that union pressures, in part supported by extensive job protection legislation, have raised the cost of employment in the formal sector. In addition, many educated job seekers appear to prefer employment in the public sector, further stifling the development of a productive formal private sector.

- Job protection regulation. Before the reform of the labor code in 1990, dismissal of workers was only possible in severe disciplinary cases. The new law permits labor shedding for economic reasons, but only after collective negotiations, arbitrated by labor inspectors, have failed to find an alternative solution. After shedding labor, employers are not allowed to take on new recruits at similar grades. Through 1994, dismissed workers were entitled to severance pay equivalent to one month's pay for each year of service up to a maximum of 15 months. Despite far-reaching reforms introduced since 1994, including the overhaul of the severance payments and unemployment insurance system (see below), the current regulations still contribute to Algeria's high unemployment: by creating incentives for insiders to ask for higher-than-market clearing wages; and by raising the cost of dismissal, thereby inducing employers to hire low-risk workers with a good work history, thus limiting the prospects for the young to find a job in the formal sector.

- Large informal sector.[25] Job protection legislation, minimum wage legislation, and sectoral or national wage agreements only cover the formal sector, and their existence has contributed to the development of the informal sector. In 1991, for example, only an estimated 27 percent of all private sector workers were salaried employees covered by the minimum wage. Labor market legislation and official wage settlements are likely to be important for the informal sector as well. As most informal activities take place within sectors of relatively low productivity (e.g., services), the availability of a few secure and well-paid jobs in the formal sector may raise unemployment by inducing workers to "line up" for them. For instance, university graduates may prefer to wait for a "lifetime" job in the public sector.

- Educational and geographical mismatches. Algeria suffers from an educational mismatch, with too many school graduates trained in the social sciences and thus better suited to join the public sector. Private sector needs have not been taken into account in the education system, and a major reorientation of labor training is required. Moreover, job intermediation continues to be inefficient. Only since 1990 have employers been free to hire as they choose, and all vacancies need to be registered with the public employment agency (Agence Nationale de l'Emploi (ANEM)). The role of ANEM has declined in recent years, and firms have increasingly developed their own recruitment channels. Geographical mismatches are also prevalent: according to a survey from the early 1990s, one-fourth of the unemployed still would not move to another province to get a job, although the share of unemployed who would accept a job of lower qualification, or in another sector or region, has increased somewhat since 1989. In addition, the housing shortage has imposed a severe constraint on labor mobility.

Labor Market Reform

Structural reforms of the labor market are an essential component of any employment-generating

---

[24]The use of capital-intensive techniques was encouraged by the overvalued exchange rate and negative real interest rates.

[25]The formal sector of the Algerian labor market comprises public sector and private sector firms with 10 or more employees, while the informal sector is made up of small firms as well as the self- and home-employed.

growth strategy. These reforms need in particular to promote employment in the formal sector because of its higher productivity and focus on the production of tradable goods. A reform agenda aimed at lowering unemployment and fostering employment in the formal sector should include the following elements:

First, further reform of job protection legislation is needed to facilitate labor shedding, provided sufficient advance notice is given. The cost of labor shedding for employers should be reduced by lowering their contribution to severance pay and by relying more on the recently introduced unemployment insurance scheme under which employers and workers would pool costs and risks. Compensation under this scheme should be limited to a shorter time period to foster an intensive job search and avoid subsidizing long-term unemployment.

Second, the legal minimum wage should serve only to protect the weaker segments in the population and not as a benchmark for the wage structure. The recent delinking of the civil service wage increases from wage increases in public enterprises, with the latter being determined in light of their individual financial situation, is a step in the right direction. A prudent minimum wage policy is all the more important, as payroll taxes in the formal sector are substantial.[26] Such taxes further exacerbate the shift of unskilled workers into the informal sector.

Third, measures are needed to reduce the high youth unemployment rate and foster employment of the young in the formal sector. The applicability of all job protection and minimum wage legislation could be limited to individuals older than 30 years. As a first step, the 1989 Finance Law introduced a series of exemptions to wage taxes applicable to the employment of youth up to age 30. This could be complemented by removing the minimum wage requirement for a period of apprenticeship.

Fourth, reforms in the educational system are needed, so as to adjust the skill profile toward the private sector. For example, labor-market entrants need to be provided with more market-relevant, technical skills, and formal apprenticeship schemes.[27]

Further reforms of the labor market and a continued restrained incomes policy to make economic growth more labor intensive would render more likely the "high-elasticity outcomes" discussed above. Robust growth in the construction sector to alleviate the housing shortage, in particular, could contribute substantially to further raising the labor intensity of GDP. Strong emphasis on labor-intensive activities (e.g., housing and agriculture) by providing the necessary institutional support would help raise employment elasticities with respect to investment over time. At the same time, strong and credible reform policies may help Algeria to achieve growth well above 6 percent, which even in the presence of relatively low elasticities would help generate faster employment gains.

Overhauling the Social Safety Net

The 1994 reform program involved substantial modifications to the safety net, with the introduction of two new elements: (1) a self-targeted public works program to substitute for the generalized subsidies, which were gradually being eliminated, and for the transfers to persons without income, which were not well targeted; and (2) an unemployment insurance system to facilitate industrial restructuring. At the same time, the government started incorporating explicitly in the budget the implicit subsidies to the housing sector.

Subsidy Reform

Generalized food and energy subsidies were costly, wasteful, and inequitable, since they were disproportionately benefiting higher income groups. First, generalized subsidies were expensive, amounting to 4 percent of GDP in 1990.[28] In addition, energy subsidies, in the form of forgone profit transfers to the treasury from the oil production and refining companies, amounted to another 4 percent of GDP. Second, the system was inefficient inasmuch as there were large leakages of income transfers to the middle class. Moreover, subsidized products were diverted toward unintended uses, and those subsidized goods that could easily be transported (e.g., powdered milk, semolina, and petroleum products) were smuggled to neighboring countries.

The expenditure of the Compensation Fund rose sharply as a result of the Algerian dinar depreciation

---

[26]According to a recent World Bank report, social security contributions in Algeria amount to 20–30 percent of the wage bill; adding other nonwage costs, the share rises to 30–50 percent.

[27]The existing apprenticeship scheme is not supported by formal curriculums or degrees. It might be possible to take certain elements of the German apprenticeship scheme, which provides young men and women with nationally recognized degrees that are obtained through practical work within a firm as well as attendance of a post-secondary school.

[28]Subsidies on certain items (mostly food) were paid out of a special treasury extrabudgetary account, the Compensation Fund, which paid enterprises the difference between the import cost of the products and their controlled prices. This fund was financed by three sources of revenues: (1) budgetary transfers; (2) earmarked levies on imports and on domestic production in the form of compensatory taxes; and (3) other exceptional levies on domestic sales.

VI THE SOCIAL DIMENSION OF ADJUSTMENT

> **Box 8. Structure of Unemployment**
>
> In Algeria, as in most North African countries, the unemployed are mainly under 25 years old, typically remain unemployed for more than one year, mostly live in urban areas, and tend to have at least a secondary education. Moreover, female unemployment is widespread. This points to labor market rigidities that would need to be addressed.
>
> *High urban unemployment.* The proportion of labor force participants that are self-employed has been rising steadily, accounting for one-fourth of all employed in 1991. As the self-employed almost by definition cannot become unemployed, the aggregate unemployment rate reflects pressures on labor markets only imperfectly. As self-employment and unpaid family employment are particularly large in agriculture, it is estimated that urban unemployment rates are even higher than the national average.
>
> *Geographical mismatches.* For both social and economic reasons, geographical mismatches are prevalent. People are generally reluctant to move to another province to get a job, and their ability to do so remains highly constrained by the acute housing shortage.
>
> *High youth unemployment.* The unemployment rate among the young is nearly twice the global rate, in line with the situation in many Mediterranean countries. In 1991, about 41 percent of the labor force aged 20–25 were unemployed. The likelihood of being unemployed falls rapidly with age, and among the labor force aged 30 and older, only 6 percent were unemployed. Given the large share of youth in the total labor force, this implies that the bulk of the unemployed are under 25 years old, raising major social and political concerns, in part because of the weakness of the social safety net.
>
> *Educational mismatches.* Unemployment data broken down by educational background indicate that unemployment rates do not necessarily decline with the amount of education received. Indeed, the unemployment rate of individuals with a middle or secondary education is highest (26–30 percent in 1991). The unemployment rate is lowest among those with post-secondary education (6 percent) and those with no education (14 percent). People with primary school education may be more successful in finding the jobs of their choice. Primary school degree holders are likely to work within the informal sector, as self- or home-employed, while those with a secondary school degree line up for the few formal sector jobs, notably the secure jobs in public administration. As recruitment in the public sector slowed down during the second half of the 1980s, graduates had to wait longer before being offered a job. Furthermore, a large share of graduates may have had degrees in the social sciences, and their job opportunities in the private sector were therefore more limited.
>
> *Long unemployment duration.* Recent data on the proportion of long-term unemployed—for more than one year—in total unemployment are not available. Based on labor surveys, the average length of unemployment spells was 23 months in 1991; by age, the average length of unemployment peaked for the age group 25–34 at 36 months, and was longer for men than for women. The long-term unemployed are likely to be much younger in Algeria.

during 1990 and, in early 1991, the authorities introduced several measures to reduce the number, scope, and extent of subsidies (see Box 9). The subsidy system, however, continued to involve distortions and large costs to the government and remained poorly targeted.[29] These distortions and the need to reduce the budget deficit set the stage for a further reduction in subsidies. In June 1992, administered prices for food items were increased. As a result, the budgetary cost of food subsidies declined from the equivalent of 4 percent of GDP in 1990 to 2.3 percent of GDP in 1992. Subsequent increases in the import cost of these commodities raised subsidies to 2.5 percent of GDP in 1993, because of the lack of a pass-through mechanism for administered prices.

To shield the poor from the 1992 adjustment to administered prices for food, the authorities introduced in February 1992 a system of transfers that provided cash allowances to four types of beneficiaries: low-income earners and their children, pensioners, and persons without income. By 1993, this scheme covered more than 60 percent of the population and cost about 2 percent of GDP. Its main weakness was that it was poorly targeted due to inadequate means-testing. Indeed, for low-income earners and their children and pensioners, targeting was based solely on the records of the Social Security Administration. Targeting was also deficient in the case of persons without income. Beneficiaries were only required to register their need and to "declare on their honor" that they did not have any source of income; ad hoc verifications would be carried out in certain cases, using the records of various agencies, such as the Tax Department, the Social Security Administration, or the Chamber of Commerce. Because

---

[29]A larger fraction of subsidies accrued to consumers belonging to the upper deciles of the income distribution, reflecting their larger consumption: consumption of rice and flour by the top percentile was 5 times greater than that of the bottom decile; the ratio was 4 for bread, 3 for table oil, 2 for pasta and lentils, and 1.5 for semolina. See Michel Lazare, Ehtisham Ahmad, and Jean-Luc Schneider, "Options pour la Réforme de la Protection Sociale," Fiscal Affairs Department Technical Assistance Report (Washington: International Monetary Fund, February 1994).

a large number of informal sector activities and intrahousehold transfers were not captured, these attempts at targeting proved inadequate with the result that 25 percent of the population were considered "without income" and benefited from cash transfers.

Beginning in 1994, cash compensation and the remaining generalized subsidies were gradually replaced by targeted transfers and subsidies. By the end of 1996, the phase-out of generalized food subsidies was completed. By the end of 1997, the overall subsidy on gas and electricity was completely eliminated, through quarterly increases in their prices (see Box 9).

Public Works Program

To partially substitute for both the generalized subsidies, which were gradually being eliminated, and the allowance paid to persons without income, which was not well targeted, a self-targeted public works program, managed at the local level, was introduced in October 1994. It was designed to provide compensation to those able to work (*Indemnité d'activités d'intérêt général*—IAIG) and to provide financial support to those unable to work (*Allocation forfaitaire de solidarité*—AFS). Those willing to work can be hired at about one-half the minimum wage—in community-based activities, such as reforestation, water works, and street cleaning. The low remuneration is designed to ensure self-targeting of those with a low opportunity cost. Those unable to work—pensioners and the disabled—receive DA 900 a month, plus DA 120 for each dependent up to a maximum of three. The public works program appeared most appropriate under the circumstances, given the pressing problem of youth unemployment and the previous unsuccessful experience with targeting.[30] On account of improved targeting, benefits to those eligible under the new system are higher than under the old system.[31] Because Algeria had experimented with community-based public works in the past, these activities could be designed and implemented quickly.[32]

A recently conducted survey indicates that the public works program has been quite successful. By the fourth quarter of 1996, there were 500,000 participants under the scheme, working for an average of eight weeks. In addition, 277,000 elderly and disabled persons participated in the cash compensation scheme, bringing the total number of participants to 7 percent of the population, and indicating that the scheme operates under substantially improved targeting. In 1997, the IAIG was supplemented by a more structured public works program supported by the World Bank and aimed at improving rural infrastructure through the creation of 20,000 yearly jobs.

Reform of Unemployment Insurance

A major reform of the unemployment insurance system was implemented in July 1994. Before the reform, enterprises were required to provide severance payments of one month of salary for each year of service to retrenched workers, paid as a lump sum at the time of layoff. Although not particularly high compared to other countries, these severance obligations in cash were onerous for enterprises in financial distress and acted as an impediment to restructuring and labor shedding.

Under the new system, retrenched workers receive a lump sum severance payment limited to three months and are not eligible for unemployment benefits during that time, to encourage active job search. Employers have to pay an "entry fee" to the Unemployment Insurance Fund (equal to 0.8 month of salary for each year of service of the retrenched worker in excess of three years, up to a maximum of 12 months) at the time of layoff. The new scheme alleviates the burden of effecting layoffs in two ways. First, it lowers the amount of severance pay by reducing compensation for employees with 3–15 years of service.[33] Second, the entry fee can be paid in monthly installments over one year. An additional advantage of the new scheme is that the small lump-sum payment and ineligibility to benefits during the first three months of unemployment encourage search behavior; it also encourages the creation of small enterprises, the most dynamic area of the Algerian private sector.

In addition to entry rights, the Unemployment Insurance Fund collects a monthly unemployment insurance contribution of 1.5 percent of the salary base from employees and 2.5 percent from employers. These payroll contributions serve to finance monthly unemployment benefits to which retrenched workers become entitled after three months. Unemployment benefits are based on a reference salary of the average

---

[30]See Ehtisham Ahmad and Philippe Marciniak, "Algeria: Social Safety Nets and Protecting the Vulnerable," Fiscal Affairs Department Technical Assistance Report (Washington: International Monetary Fund, October, 1991).

[31]The three other cash transfers were integrated into salaries, family allowances, and pensions, thus eliminating the burden of administrating these schemes on the government. To keep enterprise contributions (including social security contributions) unchanged, the budget took over the cost of the family allowance scheme.

[32]Some public works, included in the Youth Employment Program, recruited young job seekers for short periods (six to nine months) at the minimum wage, and created about 40,000 temporary jobs annually.

[33]For employees with 15 years or more, the total severance payment received is equivalent to 15 months of salary, as under the original system. Under the new system, however, the average amount of compensation received has gone down from the equivalent of 12.5 months of salary to about 12.3 months of salary, assuming a uniformly distributed labor force and a worklife of 45 years.

VI THE SOCIAL DIMENSION OF ADJUSTMENT

Box 9. Reform of the Price System and Elimination of Subsidies

Prior to 1994, the domestic price system in Algeria was subject to numerous controls and distortions. The price law of 1989 divided products into (1) those with administered prices;[1] (2) those subject to controlled profit margins;[2] and (3) those for which prices were free but still needed to be declared to the authorities. Generalized subsidies were also provided to consumers for energy products and 15 major food staples; and to producers of several agricultural products and inputs. Aside from the misallocation of resources, which this system entailed, it was also inequitable since the richer half of the population were consuming more than 60 percent of the subsidized food items. Since 1994, domestic prices have been almost entirely liberalized, with most controls on prices and profit margins lifted, and most subsidies eliminated.

Lifting of controls on prices and profit margins. A major step was taken in April 1994, through the abolition of controls on profit margins for most commodities.[3] Price controls remained only for three subsidized essential food staples (flour, semolina, and milk), energy products, and public transportation fares. Later in 1994, prices of agricultural inputs and construction prices for social housing were liberalized, and all remaining controls on profit margins[4] and prices were eliminated during the 1995/96 program year (April 1, 1995–March 31, 1996), except for medicines and subsidized food and energy products.

Elimination of generalized subsidies. Reform of the domestic price system also entailed major increases in the prices of subsidized products toward their opportunity costs. Prices of subsidized food and energy products were doubled in 1994/95 and increased by 60 percent in 1995/96. As a result of these price adjustments, subsidies were eliminated on petroleum products (October 1994), powdered milk and semolina (June 1995), regular flour (October 1995), and bread flour (January 1996). By the end of 1996, all food subsidies had been phased out. For energy products, the implicit subsidy was eliminated by setting the transfer price of crude oil from Sonatrach to the refineries at world price level, with adjustments to the transfer price every six months in line with export prices and exchange rate developments. There also remains a global subsidy on gas and electricity products (equivalent to 0.4 percent of GDP in 1996), which the government is committed to eliminate by the end of 1997. The system of quarterly revisions of the prices of electricity and gas introduced in August 1994 should prevent the reemergence of this global subsidy after the end of 1997. Nevertheless, subsidies of gas and electricity to poor households—which can be targeted through consumption levels—will continue.

Adoption of a Competition Law in January 1995, institutionalizing the principle of free price setting for all products while introducing safeguards against possible abuses by monopolistic suppliers, including through antitrust regulations. The law prohibits noncompetitive practices, such as the imposition of limits on market access or collusion between enterprises to control a particular market. This regulatory framework is being enforced by a number of institutions, including a National Competition Council, the Ministry of Commerce, and the Ministry of Justice.

---

[1]Beyond explicitly subsidized items, this category included cereals, water, gas, electricity, fuel, transportation fares, harbor services, construction costs, and cement.

[2]This category included tea, coffee, milk, metal cans for food preservation, plastic sheets for agricultural use, agricultural equipment and parts, fertilizers, lubricants, yeast, cattle feed, notebooks, textbooks and school furniture, medicines, powdered sugar, edible oils, tomato concentrate, medical instruments, furniture, equipment and materials, tobacco products and matches, semolina, high-grade flour, and pasta.

[3]Controls on profit margins were eliminated in mid-1995 for sugar, cereal grains (other than hard and soft wheat), and edible oils, and at the end of 1995 for textbooks and other school supplies.

[4]Except for edible oils, sugar, medicines, school supplies, coffee and tobacco, and five cereal products that were transferred from the category of goods with administered prices to that of goods with controlled profit margins.

---

of the gross monthly salary and the minimum wage, the SNMG. The duration of benefits equals two months for each year of contribution to the Unemployment Insurance Fund while at the last employer, with a maximum of 36 months. The eligible period for benefits is divided equally into four periods, with benefits declining gradually over these periods: from 100 percent of the reference salary in the first period, to 80 percent in the second period, 60 percent in the third period, and 50 percent in the fourth period (subject to a minimum benefit of 75 percent of SNMG and a maximum of three times the SNMG).[34] World Bank simulations show that the new unemployment insurance system would be financially viable even at current unemployment rates.

Housing Reform: Fostering a Market-Driven Supply Response

Housing needs have increased considerably in Algeria since independence in 1962, mainly as a result of rapid population growth and a high pace of urbanization (see Box 10). Housing supply has lagged behind demand, as the housing sector remained overwhelmingly dominated by inefficient state-owned construction enterprises, public real

---

[34]Assuming a uniform distribution of tenure and a worklife of 45 years, the average duration of benefits is 29.6 months.

Housing Reform: Fostering a Market-Driven Supply Response

> **Box 10. Housing**
>
> - Housing supply in Algeria has fallen short of the needs of a rapidly increasing population in Algeria, giving rise to a serious social problem, whose solution remains an important government priority. The housing stock is estimated at about 4 million units for a population of about 29 million, one of the highest occupancy ratios of the world. Moreover, the housing stock is of poor quality, with half of the dwellings over 35 years old. This, coupled with below market rents, has exerted increasing pressures on the budget. The housing shortage has stemmed essentially from the combination of a dysfunctional and cumbersome state-organized market with inefficient state-owned construction companies, poorly managed real state companies (OPGIs), and a public savings and housing financial institution unable to play properly its intermediation role.
>
> - Over the period covered by the program supported by the extended arrangement, the government took several steps to streamline its interventions, liberalize the sector, and ensure greater efficiency in the construction of public housing. In the early stages of reform, the government—in an attempt to establish market mechanisms and eliminate distortions—lifted trade and payment restrictions on imported inputs and liberalized the price of construction. At the same time, to minimize budgetary costs, the government started adjusting rents gradually, with the goal of reflecting construction costs better. However, even after sharp increases, including 30 percent in 1997 and again about 20 percent expected for 1998, rents in public housing remain well below market prices. Nonetheless, since January 1998, all new units delivered have been rented at a higher rate.
>
> - The government has initiated a progressive withdrawal from direct involvement in construction and taken actions to improve efficiency and reduce costs in its interventions in the provision of social housing. As a result, a large number of state-owned construction companies have been liquidated with about 80,000 workers dismissed as of December 1997. Meanwhile, the number of property management and promotion agencies (OPGIs) was progressively reduced from 53 in 1996 to 43 at the end of 1997, and is to be reduced to 25 by the end of 1998. In addition, in 1997, a Cost Reduction Commission was created to ensure that public projects are carried out at minimum cost. An assistance program has been elaborated to improve the targeting of social housing; however, the need to collect reliable data on household income has delayed the implementation of this mechanism. Finally, the allocation of public housing is now the full responsibility of the communes (instead of the OPGIs), which can judge better the needs of the local population, hence leading to a more just allocation of social housing.
>
> - The financial framework in place was a mayor impediment to help develop a private construction sector and, thus, stimulate the adequate supply response for the massive shortfall in housing. In response, the government began a far-reaching overhaul of the mechanisms for housing financing. In 1997, the Caisse nationale d'épargne et de prévoyance (CNEP) acquired the status of a bank and was recapitalized so as to revitalize its role of intermediary in the sector, given that it mobilizes a significant portion of household savings. At the same time, new auxiliary financial institutions were created to open housing finance to the entire banking sector and to better control related risks. To this end, a mortgage refinancing company ("Société de refinancement hypothécaire"), a mortgage guarantee company ("Société de garantie du crédit immobilier"), and a fund to provide guarantees to housing companies ("Fonds de garantie et de caution mutuelle de la promotion immobilière") were created. These institutions are expected to become fully functional in the course of 1998, after the operating mechanisms have been put into place with foreign technical assistance. The capital of these new institutions was provided essentially by the banking sector.
>
> - The 1997 government program called for an acceleration of the public construction program. Out of 142,000 units approved in 1995 under the previous social construction program (PEC), about 79,000 had been delivered by the end of 1997, and the remainder is to be delivered in 1998. In addition, the supplementary budget for 1998 envisages a new PEC of 80,000 units including 20,000 that were started at the end of 1997. About 5,000 of these new constructions are expected to be delivered in 1998, and construction will be performed by both private and public contractors. The contribution of the budget to public housing amounts to DA 80 billion (2.8 percent of GDP) in 1998. Also, a joint program with the World Bank to deal with the problem of shanty towns will be launched by the end of 1998 with a total contribution of $200 million.

estate management companies, and a state-owned housing financial institution (CNEP). Long and costly delays for housing completion plagued the sector, particularly in the early 1990s, when imports of construction inputs were curtailed as a result of foreign exchange rationing. Provision of subsidized public housing covered a broad income group and was mostly given out to public sector employees. While the deposit base of the CNEP was channeled to finance public rental housing, financing for unsubsidized private housing was virtually nonexistent. As a result, Algeria has a severe housing shortage that has largely contributed to social discontent in recent years. With a housing stock of low average quality and of less than 4 million units for a population of more than 28 million, it has one of the highest occupancy ratios in the world (Figure 8).

VI THE SOCIAL DIMENSION OF ADJUSTMENT

Because of past centralized planning and rent control, the supply of housing has come mostly from the public sector. Almost 50 percent of the housing units delivered by the formal sector between 1980 and 1996 consisted of state-owned rental units. Housing supply has traditionally been heavily subsidized through a system of administered controls keeping construction prices, rents of public housing, and mortgage rates below market-clearing levels.

The system of implicit subsidization of housing resulted in mounting losses—financed by banks—for construction companies and public rental agencies, and produced only a limited supply of housing that has not reached the neediest segments of the population. Since 1994, this system has been gradually phased out and replaced by a system in which (1) subsidies on construction inputs and administered prices on construction costs have been eliminated; (2) most housing is supplied by the private sector at market prices; and (3) government subsidies for housing are explicitly budgeted and redirected toward those who otherwise could not afford housing. This change in strategy, which is expected to foster a substantial market-driven increase in housing supply, requires the restructuring of the housing construction sector, a reform of the rental housing market, and the revamping of housing finance.

Restructuring the Housing Construction Sector

Algeria had a large number of inefficient public construction enterprises that employed about 240,000 workers in 1994 and accounted for more than 80 percent of the total value added of the construction sector. The restructuring of the sector was initiated in 1992 with the support of the World Bank Enterprise and Financial Sector Adjustment Loan, and was accelerated first in 1994 with the liberalization of imports of construction materials and construction prices, and since 1995, through various measures aiming at both hardening budget constraints faced by public enterprises and increasing participation of the private sector in the supply of housing. In particular, public construction companies have been granted autonomy while nonviable ones are being liquidated. By 1997, numerous public construction companies had been liquidated. The workforce of public construction enterprises has been reduced and most labor contracts were transformed from full-time employment to contractual employment. In this context, about 93,000 workers were laid off in 1995–97, or 51 percent of the current employment in public construction companies. Finally, public enterprises have increased recourse to private subcontractors in the finishing stages of construction. To this end, contracts for public housing projects were parceled out into small components, more in line with the capacity of private contractors.

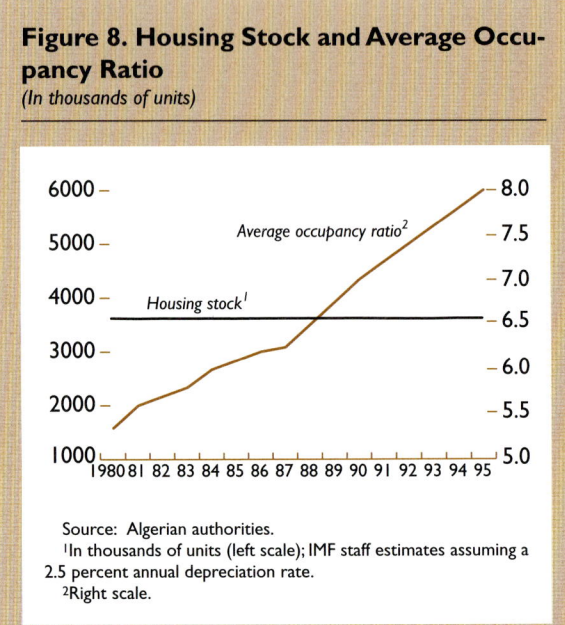

Figure 8. Housing Stock and Average Occupancy Ratio
(In thousands of units)

Source: Algerian authorities.
[1] In thousands of units (left scale); IMF staff estimates assuming a 2.5 percent annual depreciation rate.
[2] Right scale.

As a result of these actions, the participation of the private sector in the construction of public housing for rent has increased from 20 percent in 1994 to more than 50 percent in 1997. The number of formal construction projects for sale launched by the private sector is estimated to have increased by more than 50 percent since 1994. The increased involvement of small private construction firms has also contributed to a decline in the completion period for more than five years to one year for some projects, which, in turn, has translated into a substantial fall in construction costs.

Overall, yearly housing deliveries by the formal sector are estimated to have increased from 82,000 units in 1994 to 130,000 units in 1996 (Figure 9). The increase mostly occurred in public housing and stemmed from efforts at finishing dwellings launched prior to the 1994 adjustment program. The stock of ongoing construction projects at the end of 1996 was estimated at 170,000 units, including 110,000 units of public housing for rent. The latter could be completed in about two years assuming that the pace of housing deliveries is maintained at the level achieved in 1995 and 1996. As part of the shift from rental public housing to the promotion of owner-occupied housing, however, these completed units will be sold.

Over the next few years, restructuring of the housing sector will require an acceleration of the liquidation of nonviable public construction enterprises and the privatization of others. As shown by the recent

Housing Reform: Fostering a Market-Driven Supply Response

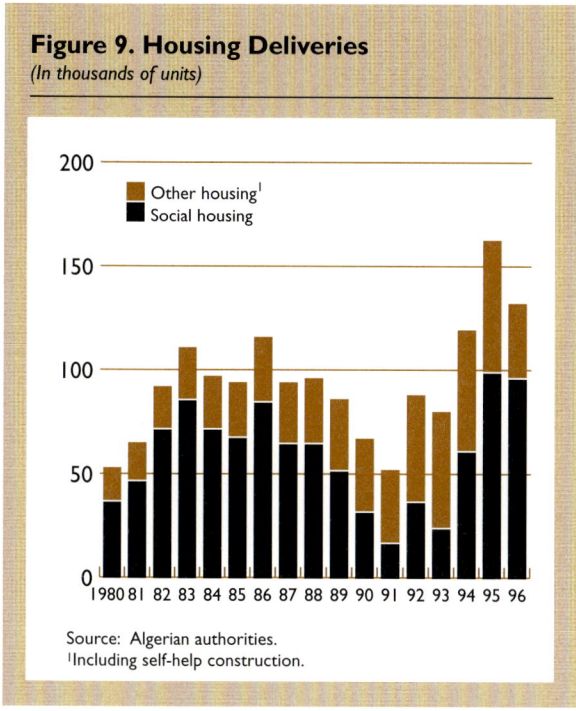

Figure 9. Housing Deliveries
(In thousands of units)

Source: Algerian authorities.
[1]Including self-help construction.

experience of the transition economies of eastern Europe, privatizing housing construction can quickly lead to significant productivity gains as this activity is particularly suited for small- to medium-scale enterprises. Many aspects of housing construction are relatively labor-intensive and can be easily subcontracted to small enterprises organized into specialized guilds. The possibility of privatization in the construction sector is, therefore, not as dependent on the availability of foreign direct investment as that of other more capital-intensive sectors in the Algerian economy.

Reforming the Housing Rental Market

The supply of rental housing in Algeria has been almost exclusively provided by the government through public rental companies (OPGIs) at rent well below market-clearing levels. At the end of 1996, rents for a publicly owned, two-bedroom city apartment, ranged from $8 to $12, while private sector rents for similar dwellings ranged from $55 to $85. In 1996, rents actually collected by the OPGIs were still only about 40 percent of rents due, and covered less than 70 percent of personnel and maintenance costs. Moreover, public rental housing was made accessible to a broad spectrum of middle-income tenants, including a large segment of public sector employees.

Several measures were implemented in 1996 to remedy the structural causes of financial imbalances of the OPGIs. Specifically, the Civil and Penal Codes were amended with a view to placing the burden of proof of rental payments on tenants and allowing the licensing of private property managers. In the context of this new legal framework, the government, in 1997/98, will proceed to restructure viable OPGIs and liquidate loss-making ones. The restructuring process will entail the privatization of the existing stock of public housing for rent as well as the subcontracting of its maintenance to the private sector. As a result of the transfer of these functions to the private sector, remaining OPGIs will only retain a limited staff to perform their role as contractors for public housing programs.

Concurrently, subsidized public rents were increased substantially between March 1994 and December 1997. The idea is to gradually raise rents for public housing to market levels, while putting in place a system of well-targeted and fully budgetized direct subsidies to low-income tenants. During the transition period, any loss made by OPGIs will be accounted for in the government budget. These measures should facilitate the purchase of state-owned apartments by their tenants and contribute to the development of a private rental market for housing.

Revamping Housing Finance

Housing finance in Algeria has de facto been monopolized by the state-owned housing fund (CNEP). Although commercial banks are legally allowed to extend mortgage financing to households, the CNEP was the only financial institution providing mortgage loans at preferential interest rates to holders of saving accounts. The number of concessional mortgage loans was limited by the availability of housing and benefited the better-off depositors who could meet the CNEP's prescribed interest accumulation threshold. In addition, as noted earlier, most of the savings of the CNEP's depositors were channeled to OPGIs to finance public housing for rent. The inability of OPGIs to service their debt with the CNEP has caused severe liquidity problems for the CNEP, particularly after 1995, when it depleted its stock of treasury bonds after having faced a stagnant depositor base under the old negative interest rate structure.

This situation has called for a major overhaul of housing finance on the basis of the following principles: (1) there must be a clear separation of the subsidization of housing and mortgage financing; (2) all banks should be in a position to participate, on a competitive basis, in the supply of mortgage loans; and (3) mortgage loans must be supported by clearly defined property rights to ensure that they can actually be recovered.

With the first principle, the government has decided to channel all public subsidies to housing as

VI THE SOCIAL DIMENSION OF ADJUSTMENT

well as finance any new public housing project exclusively through the budget. The government also restructured the CNEP into a housing bank operating solely on a commercial basis in early 1997. To this end, in April 1997, government recapitalized the CNEP and took over all the OPGI's nonperformance debt to the CNEP in exchange for government bonds. Interest rates on CNEP deposits were increased significantly over the last two years, resulting in a substantial growth of deposits in 1996–97.

To facilitate the broadening of mortgage financing to all commercial banks, a mortgage refinancing institution was created in 1997. This new institution will deal only with other financial institutions and will allow commercial banks to participate in the mortgage market while keeping the maturity structure of their assets in line with that of their liabilities.

Finally, regarding property rights, a major operation has been launched since 1993 to update and extend the coverage of the national land registry. This process, which is expected to be completed by 2008, should be accelerated to strengthen the legal basis for property registration. In addition, the availability of land for construction purposes will be increased as a result of a land privatization law, which should be enacted in 1998.

VII External Sector Developments

External developments have always played a key role in Algeria's economy owing to the dominant role of the hydrocarbon sector, which contributes a large share of budget revenue, and whose exports have generally accounted for more than 95 percent of total export receipts. Changes in the external environment and domestic economic policies have, therefore, remained closely intertwined. Persistent domestic financial imbalances in the late 1980s hindered attempts to liberalize external transactions and gave rise to an overvalued exchange rate and mounting external debt as unsustainable absorption levels were financed by borrowing abroad. Escalating debt service costs precipitated the withdrawal of external financing in the face of a looming balance of payments crisis at the end of 1993, which, in turn, was one of the key factors behind the authorities' decision to implement a drastic adjustment program. Since a realignment of relative prices and price liberalization were the cornerstone of the reform package launched in 1994, the latter was accompanied by a large up-front devaluation and included broad trade and exchange rate liberalization measures. These steps had widespread repercussions on the financial position of enterprises and banks, and on the budget balance, which had to be addressed in the context of structural reforms. This section examines external developments since the mid-1980s, as well as different aspects of external policies and their role in the overall reform process.

Balance of Payments Developments

Developments Until 1994

Up until the mid-1980s, high oil prices had allowed Algeria to finance high domestic absorption. The dramatic fall in oil prices in 1986, however, highlighted emerging domestic macroeconomic imbalances and the country's vulnerability. Algeria's crude oil export price fell by one-half between 1985 and 1986, and total export revenues declined by 38 percent (see Figures 10, 11, and 12). In response, although the authorities stepped up borrowing, they had to resort to import restrictions and, between 1985 and 1987, imports declined by 43 percent in real terms. State enterprises,

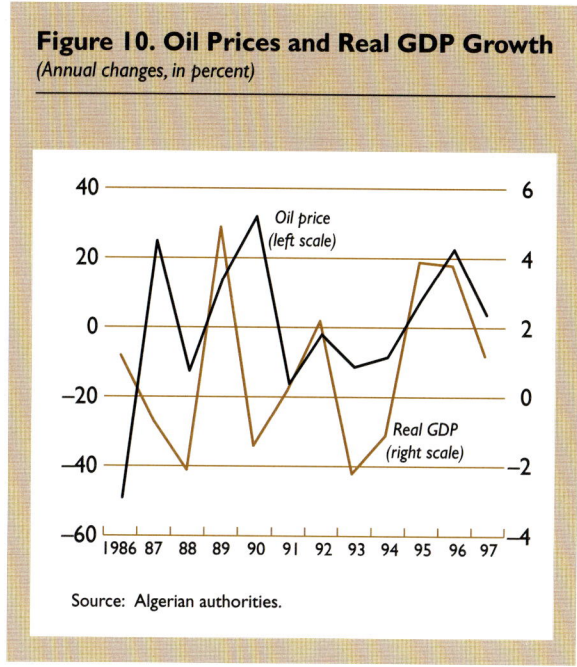

Figure 10. Oil Prices and Real GDP Growth
(Annual changes, in percent)

Source: Algerian authorities.

unable to purchase needed supplies, ran into difficulties, and strong incentives for the emergence of a parallel foreign exchange market were generated.

Although oil prices recovered gradually by 1990, and rose sharply during the 1991 Gulf crisis, Algeria made an effort to move to a more open, market-driven economy, and entered into two financing arrangements with the IMF in 1989 and 1991. Both programs were accompanied by a purchase under the IMF's Compensatory and Contingency Financing Facility[35] on account of fluctuations in exports and the cost of cereal imports.[36]

---

[35]The Compensatory and Contingency Financing Facility is an IMF loan facility that provides financial assistance to members experiencing temporary shortfalls in export earnings and temporary excesses in cereal import costs attributable to circumstances beyond members' control.

[36]The 1991 Compensatory and Contingency Financing Facility was in the form of an external contingency financing mechanism to be drawn in the event of lower oil prices. It was not activated, and the final review of the 1991 Stand-By Arrangement was not completed.

VII External Sector Developments

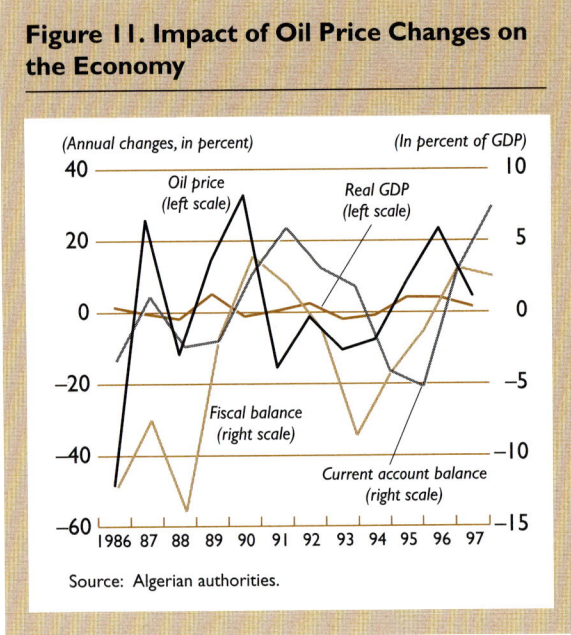

Figure 11. Impact of Oil Price Changes on the Economy

Source: Algerian authorities.

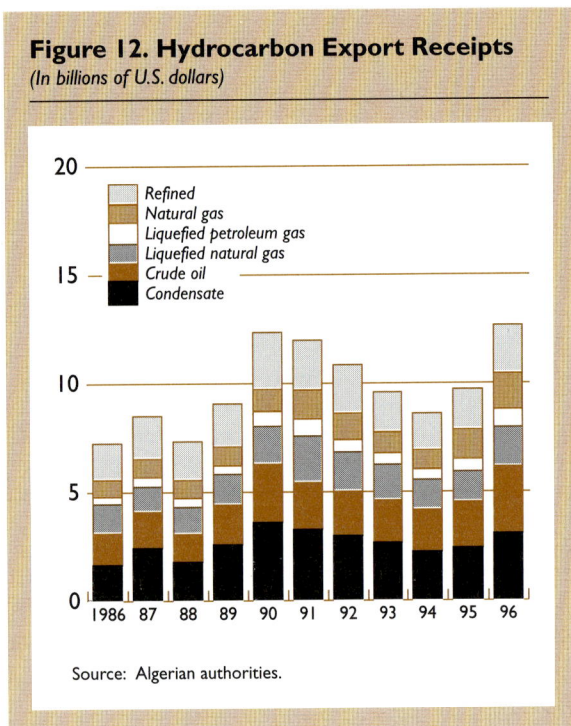

Figure 12. Hydrocarbon Export Receipts
(In billions of U.S. dollars)

Source: Algerian authorities.

In 1991, Algeria had been experiencing the effects of prolonged drought conditions, and international oil prices had begun to decline again. Algeria's balance of payments during this period was characterized by reserve losses and increased borrowing. The stock of external debt rose from $18.4 billion (about 30 percent of GDP) in 1985 to $26.5 billion (63 percent of GDP) in 1993. Not only was the increase substantial but, by 1994, the maturity profile was shortened and unevenly distributed; new borrowing—mostly from export credit agencies—had been short-term in nature (two to three years), and thereby contributed to raising the debt-service ratio from 35 percent of exports of goods and nonfactor services in 1985 to an unsustainable level of 82 percent in 1993 (see Table 9).

While efforts to improve openness had made some progress, the reform package was incomplete, and the heavy debt-service burden hindered efforts to expand productive capacity through new investment and prevented any serious recovery in growth. These circumstances set the stage for a reversal in the trend toward a more open trade regime. In 1992, trade policies reverted to past administrative practices as further explicit exchange restrictions were applied and a wider range of imports was prohibited. Growing imbalances, however, could not be contained by this approach and a foreign exchange crisis emerged at the end of 1993 when reserves had declined to below $1.5 billion (about one month of imports).[37]

Developments Since 1994

To address the crisis, a major reform initiative was launched in early 1994, supported by an IMF arrangement and comprehensive debt rescheduling. A 12-month Stand-By Arrangement in April 1994 was followed by a three-year Enhanced Fund Facility in May 1995. Both arrangements were accompanied by a Compensatory and Contingency Financing Facility purchase and Paris Club reschedulings. A rescheduling agreement with the London Club was reached and concluded in June 1996.

The external sector objectives of the authorities' program were to reduce the debt service to a sustainable level and to establish balance of payments viability by mid-1998. The key element was an up-front devaluation of the Algerian dinar and the switch from an exchange rate peg to a managed float responsive to market signals. Unlike previous occasions, the devaluation was accompanied by external assistance and appropriately supportive economic policies that enhanced its contribution to the stabilization and recovery process. These included (1) major liberalization of prices and the exchange and trade systems to realign domestic prices with world prices and provide the appropriate market incentives; (2) tight financial policies; and (3) structural reforms to establish market mechanisms and elicit a supply response. The reform strategy was designed to help relieve import shortages

---
[37]Import coverage would have been even lower relative to a noncompressed level of imports.

Balance of Payments Developments

Table 9. Balance of Payments
(In billions of U.S. dollars)

	1986	1987	1988	1989	1990	1991	1992	1993	1994	1995	1996	1997
Current account balance	−2.22	0.15	−2.04	−0.88	1.35	2.39	1.30	0.80	−1.84	−2.24	1.24	3.46
Trade balance	−0.46	1.76	−0.07	0.09	3.11	4.67	3.21	2.42	−0.26	0.16	0.12	5.69
Exports, f.o.b.	8.07	9.03	7.62	9.56	12.88	12.44	11.51	10.41	8.89	10.26	13.21	13.82
Hydrocarbons	7.82	8.81	7.21	9.16	12.35	11.97	10.98	9.88	8.61	9.73	12.64	13.18
Other	0.25	0.22	0.41	0.40	0.53	0.47	0.53	0.53	0.28	0.53	0.57	0.64
Total imports	−8.53	−7.27	−7.69	−9.47	−9.77	−7.77	−8.30	−7.99	−9.15	−10.10	−9.09	−8.13
Nonfactor services, net	−1.70	−1.20	−1.52	−0.89	−1.20	−1.35	−1.14	−1.01	−1.24	−1.33	−1.40	−1.08
Credits	0.63	0.65	0.54	0.52	0.51	0.42	0.62	0.60	0.69	0.68	0.75	1.07
Debits	−2.33	−1.85	−2.06	−1.41	−1.71	−1.77	−1.76	−1.61	−1.93	−2.01	−2.15	−2.15
Factor income, net	−1.43	−1.53	−2.01	−1.89	−2.09	−2.22	−2.16	−1.75	−1.74	−2.19	−2.36	−2.21
Credits	0.17	0.11	0.07	0.11	0.07	0.07	0.11	0.15	0.10	0.12	0.21	0.26
Debits	−1.60	−1.64	−2.08	−2.00	−2.16	−2.29	−2.27	−1.90	−1.84	−2.31	−2.56	−2.47
Transfers, net	1.37	1.12	1.56	1.81	1.53	1.29	1.39	1.14	1.40	1.12	0.88	1.06
Capital account balance	0.76	−0.42	1.23	0.24	−1.57	−1.88	−1.07	−0.81	−2.54	−4.09	−3.34	−2.29
Direct investment, net	−0.06	−0.11	−0.05	−0.03	−0.04	−0.08	0.03	0.00	0.00	0.00	0.27	0.26
Official capital, net	0.43	0.13	1.01	0.22	−0.44	−1.22	0.08	−0.33	−2.48	−3.89	−3.40	−2.51
Drawings	3.96	3.76	5.48	5.22	6.29	6.00	6.91	6.52	4.64	3.22	1.82	1.69
Amortization	−3.53	−3.63	−4.47	−5.00	−6.73	−7.22	−6.83	−6.85	−7.12	−7.11	−5.22	−4.20
Short-term credit (net) and errors and omissions	0.39	−0.44	0.27	0.05	−1.09	−0.58	−1.18	−0.48	−0.06	−0.20	−0.21	−0.04
Overall balance	−1.46	−0.27	−0.81	−0.64	−0.22	0.51	0.23	−0.01	−4.38	−6.32	−2.11	1.17
Financing	1.46	0.27	0.81	0.64	0.22	−0.51	−0.23	0.01	4.38	6.32	2.11	−1.17
Increase in gross reserves (−)	1.16	−0.01	0.79	0.06	0.09	−0.84	0.10	0.00	−1.14	0.53	−2.12	−3.82
Fund repurchases	0.00	0.00	0.00	0.00	0.00	0.00	−0.16	−0.30	−0.20	−0.17	−0.14	−0.35
Increase in other liabilities of Bank of Algeria (+)	0.00	−0.09	0.00	0.00	0.00	0.00	0.00	0.33	−0.02	−0.09	−0.11	0.00
Valuation change	0.32	0.35	0.00	0.00	0.00	0.00	0.00	0.00	0.00	0.00	0.00	0.00
Change in arrears	0.00	0.00	0.00	0.00	0.14	0.03	−0.18	0.00	0.00	0.00	0.00	0.00
Exceptional financing[1]	0.00	0.00	0.00	0.00	0.00	0.00	0.00	0.00	5.72	6.04	4.48	3.03
Rescheduling	0.00	0.00	0.00	0.00	0.00	0.00	0.00	0.00	4.49	4.94	3.53	2.22
Multilateral balance of payments support	0.00	0.00	0.00	0.00	0.00	0.00	0.00	0.00	0.38	0.63	0.20	0.34
Fund purchases	0.00	0.00	0.00	0.58	0.00	0.31	0.00	0.00	0.85	0.47	0.74	0.46
Memorandum items:												
Gross reserves (excluding gold)	1.70	1.71	0.92	0.86	0.77	1.61	1.51	1.50	2.64	2.11	4.23	8.04
In months of imports (goods and nonfactor services)	1.9	2.3	1.1	0.9	0.8	2.0	1.8	1.9	2.9	2.1	4.5	9.4
Crude oil export unit value (U.S. dollars/barrel)	14.80	18.50	16.20	18.50	24.36	20.44	20.05	17.75	16.31	17.58	21.69	19.49
Debt service after rescheduling/exports (in percent)	59.0	54.4	80.3	69.4	66.4	74.0	76.3	92.3	48.7	42.5	29.2	29.8
Total external debt[2]	21.10	24.60	24.70	26.07	26.71	26.96	26.11	26.40	29.47	32.50	33.49	30.03
Debt stock/exports (in percent)[2]	242.5	254.1	302.7	258.6	199.5	209.6	215.3	259.8	307.5	297.1	240.1	201.6
Current account/GDP (in percent)	−3.6	0.9	−2.6	−2.2	2.5	5.7	2.9	1.6	−4.4	−5.4	2.7	7.3

Sources: Data provided by the Algerian authorities; and IMF staff estimates.
[1]Does not include the *reprofilage* in 1992 of debt to commercial banks and an export credit agency.
[2]Includes short-term debt and use of IMF resources; excludes debt to Russia.

VII EXTERNAL SECTOR DEVELOPMENTS

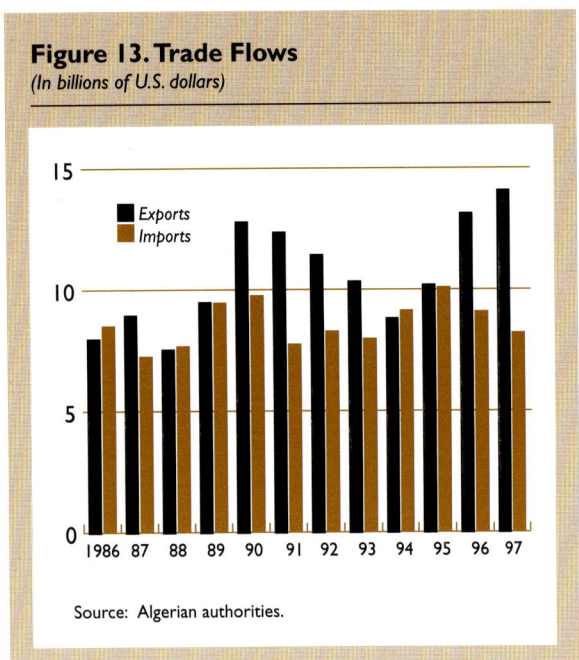

Figure 13. Trade Flows
(In billions of U.S. dollars)

Source: Algerian authorities.

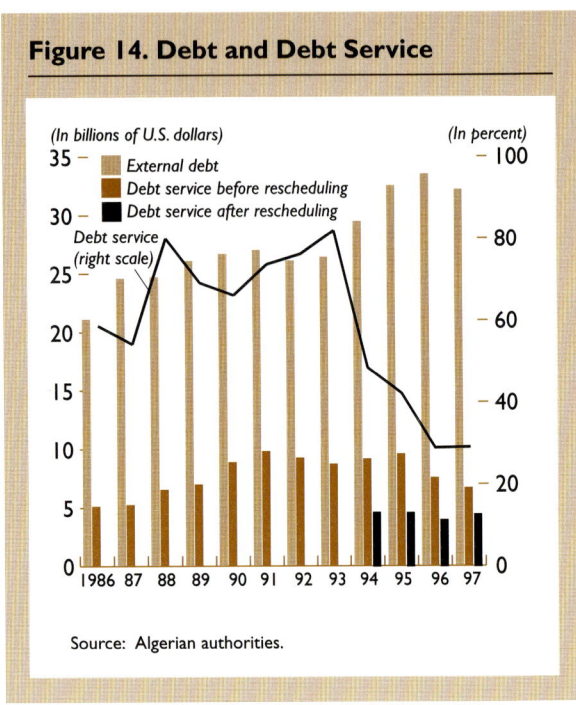

Figure 14. Debt and Debt Service

Source: Algerian authorities.

that had arisen due to administrative controls. This was achieved by accompanying trade liberalization with sufficient external financing so as to allow greater domestic absorption and preserve per capita income even in the context of the adjustment program. The external current account shifted from a surplus of 1.6 percent of GDP in 1993 to a deficit of 5.3 percent of GDP in 1995.

External conditions were adversely affected by a decline in the terms of trade in 1994 because of lower oil prices, and in 1995 because of higher cereal import costs, while external financing flows declined significantly (see Figure 13). In 1994, capital inflows were still fairly high at $4.6 billion, which, together with balance of payments support, allowed for a buildup in official reserves to three months of imports and a reduction in the debt-service burden from 82 percent of exports to 49 percent (see Figure 14). By contrast, in 1995, the increase in nonhydrocarbon imports following import liberalization measures, a severe drought, and exchange rate movements—which raised debt-service costs in U.S. dollars terms—contributed to a deterioration in the current account deficit to more than 5 percent of GDP. With little new borrowing, despite balance of payments support of $6 billion, official reserves declined by $530 million.

These trends changed radically in 1996 and 1997: while hydrocarbon export receipts advanced strongly as average oil prices surged by $4 to $21.7 a barrel, imports contracted after pent-up demand for imports was satisfied and stocks were replenished, and the current account moved into a surplus of 2.7 percent of GDP in 1996 and 7.3 percent of GDP in 1997. Despite a further decline in capital inflows to $1.8 billion, foreign reserves rose by more than $2 billion to $4.2 billion by the end of 1996, and $8 billion by the end of 1997.

Trade Policy

Trade Policy and Reforms Prior to 1994

During the 1970s and 1980s, decisions related to external trade were centrally planned.[38] The government awarded monopoly importing rights to designated public enterprises, and all other public and private firms needed prior authorization by the central bank for the payment of imported goods and services. In 1989, a gradual but significant liberalization of the trade regime was initiated (see Box 11). Centralized import controls were replaced by a more flexible system whereby firms were allocated a certain amount of foreign exchange and credit for use at their discretion. The Law on Money and Credit, adopted in April 1990, was accompanied by the Supplementary Finance Law in August 1990, which introduced a system of concessionaires and wholesalers, contributing to the breakup of the import monopolies to some degree.[39] From

---

[38] A 1978 law granted the state monopoly rights over all external transactions.

[39] Concessionaires had the right to an exclusive dealership from a foreign supplier. These entities needed the approval of the Council on Money and Credit for importing or accepting foreign investment. The system was meant to improve supply and after-sales services in the economy.

> **Box 11. Trade Regime and Foreign Exchange System—Pre-1994 Chronology of Reforms**
>
> **1988**
> - Only registered public enterprises (41) were authorized to import with foreign exchange allocated by a centralized system of import licenses; other entities needed government authorization; 100 percent of export receipts had to be surrendered immediately to the Bank of Algeria.
> - The Algerian dinar exchange rate was pegged to a basket of currencies; no interbank foreign exchange market was in existence and all foreign exchange was held at the central bank; nonresident foreigners were allowed to hold foreign currency accounts; nationals could hold foreign currency accounts with accredited institutions if the funds had been transferred from abroad or between banks; direct deposits by residents were allowed provided the funds were declared upon entry into the country.
>
> **1989**
> - Imports financed by credits in excess of 90 days required Bank of Algeria authorization; imports under $2 million had to be paid in cash or with financing terms under 90 days.
>
> **1990**
> - Imports under DA 10,000 were unrestricted; accredited importers were allowed to import certain items without restrictions using their own foreign exchange; the surrender requirement was reduced to 50 percent for agricultural exports, 20 percent for tourism receipts and wine, and 10 percent for transport, insurance, and financial services; exporters had to use their own foreign currency for authorized imports, and could only exchange it at the Bank of Algeria.
> - Companies as well as individuals were allowed to hold foreign currency accounts that could be funded by retention of foreign exchange from export activities; funds could be transferred to other foreign currency accounts or used abroad to pay for imports.
>
> **1991**
> - All entities were allowed to import for their own use or resale except goods prohibited by the state; imports of privately financed automobiles were suspended; certain strategic items (food, medicine, construction materials) were subject to controls due to domestic trading restrictions; import requests had to be channeled through accredited banks that had to try to attain financing terms over three years for capital goods and 18 months for all other imports.
> - Foreigners were allowed to hold foreign currency accounts; account holders could obtain forward contracts against currency risk from their financial institutions.
>
> **1992**
> - Imports were subject to (1) an import duty (scale of 6), (2) an ad valorem fiscal surtax, and (3) a duty surcharge of 2.4 percent; under tariff reform, international tariffs were harmonized: the number of tariff rates was reduced from 18 to 6 (0.3 percent, 7 percent, 15 percent, 25 percent, 40 percent, and 60 percent); the maximum rate was reduced from 120 percent to 60 percent, the number of exemptions was also reduced; all imports in excess of $100,000 and financed by official foreign exchange reserves had to be authorized by the Ministerial Comité Ad Hoc; imports were restricted according to the following classification: "priority," "second priority," and "prohibited."
> - Commercial banks were allowed more freedom to manage foreign exchange from export receipts; they were no longer required to submit to the central bank foreign exchange borrowed abroad or arising from nonhydrocarbon exports.

April 1991, any entity on the Algerian commercial registry became eligible to import goods for resale as a wholesaler, thereby greatly increasing competition, and importers of merchandise were given full access to foreign exchange at the official rate. All import licensing restrictions were abolished, although a few imports continued to be subject to administrative control owing to domestic trading restrictions. Each import transaction was channeled through a bank that had to help the importer find foreign credits on appropriate terms.[40] Restrictions on trade-in services—tourism, and health and education expenses abroad—remained.

In 1992, renewed financial imbalances led authorities to tighten exchange restrictions and broaden import prohibitions. In late 1992, authorities started to enforce strict rules on financing: transactions over $100,000 had to be approved by the Comité Ad Hoc, and commercial credit had to meet minimum maturity requirements ranging from 18 months to 36 months. Since trade financing on these terms was not available for imports of intermediate goods, imports were biased toward finished products. To offset this bias, authorities decreed that "nonpriority" imports would be denied access to foreign exchange.[41]

---

[40]If this quest failed, the importer could ask the Foreign Borrowing Committee to approve less favorable terms or use a foreign currency account.

[41]Imports were subdivided into three categories: (1) "priority" imports relating to strategic commodities (including food staples, medicines, construction materials, school supplies, and products necessary for the development of the hydrocarbon sector), authorized by the Ministry of Trade, with implied quotas and a pricing policy to ensure uniform domestic prices; (2) "second priority" imports, that is, goods needed to promote production and investment in strategic, high-employment industries; and (3) restricted goods, mainly luxury consumer goods (added to another list of already-prohibited consumer goods), and 60 items that could only be financed by the importers' own foreign exchange resources.

VII EXTERNAL SECTOR DEVELOPMENTS

Essentially, from the onset of the reverse oil shock in 1986 until March 1994, the government attempted to contain imports using trade and payments restrictions. As a result of these policies, import volumes in 1988 were about 30 percent lower than in 1985. After some increase in imports following the liberalization of 1989, controls and exchange restrictions were intensified again in 1992 to ensure the full servicing of external debt and protect a minimum level of foreign exchange reserves. By 1993, imports were only two-thirds of their 1985 level in real terms. Import rationing had a severe negative impact on the manufacturing and construction sectors, depriving them of needed equipment and supplies.

Trade Reforms Since 1994

The reform package launched in 1994 included broad trade liberalization measures. The removal of restrictions that began in April 1994 was executed in stages: the rule that certain consumer imports be exclusively financed by the importer's own foreign exchange was eliminated;[42] imports of used industrial and professional equipment were liberalized; minimum maturity requirements on import financing were abolished (gradually in the case of capital goods imports). To increase openness and foster regional integration, tariff protection was also reduced and maximum import tariffs were lowered first in 1996, from 60 percent to 50 percent, and then to 45 percent on January 1, 1997. Import prohibitions were limited to three categories[43] but were subsequently completely abolished by the middle of 1995. On the export side, virtually all previous export prohibitions—about 20 items—were eliminated. By June 1996, Algeria's trade system was free of quantitative restrictions.

As a result of trade liberalization, imports rose sharply in 1994 and this upward trend continued in 1995. Nonetheless, total imports in 1995 remained below the 1990 level in real terms and despite trade liberalization, imports declined in real terms in 1996 and stayed at that level in 1997. This occurred for several reasons: imports declined in 1996 after an initial surge to satisfy pent-up demand; food imports fell in the wake of an exceptional domestic agricultural harvest; and state enterprises experienced difficulties obtaining foreign financing, while domestically they became subject to increasingly hard budget constraints at a time when they suffered from more intense competition. In addition, consumer goods imports declined owing to falling real household incomes. These forces continued to exert downward pressure on import growth in 1997, although a more fundamental change in the economy's propensity to import has evolved because of the adjustment program; that is, imports as a share of GDP have declined following the closure of restructuring of inefficient, import-intensive public enterprises. Consequently, the composition of imports is also changing, and while non-oil economic activity remains weak, imports are expected to remain subdued. Over the medium term, imports are expected to grow in line with GDP and further tariff reductions are envisaged in the context of a Free Trade Agreement currently being negotiated with the European Union, as well as membership in the World Trade Organization.

Exchange Rate Policy and Exchange Restrictions

Exchange Rate Policy

From January 1974, the exchange rate of the Algerian dinar was pegged to a basket of currencies, which was adjusted from time to time. The U.S. dollar was assigned a relatively large weight in the basket due to its importance in oil export receipts and debt-service payments. The substantial appreciation of the U.S. dollar during the first half of the 1980s led to a correspondingly large rise (about 50 percent) in the real value of the Algerian dinar, thus undermining the competitiveness of nonhydrocarbon exports and stimulating imports. In 1986, Algeria's economy experienced the reverse oil shock, and the government responded to the dramatic erosion of export revenue by borrowing abroad and intensifying import restrictions. Concurrently, an active exchange rate policy was adopted, which involved a depreciation of the Algerian dinar against the basket by 31 percent between 1986 and 1988. Nevertheless, with the allocation of foreign exchange subject to a myriad of restrictions, demand for foreign exchange in the informal market grew, driving the premium in the parallel market rate to a factor of about 5.

Starting in 1988, this rigid system was replaced by a system of foreign exchange allocation to the five public commercial banks within the framework of credit ceilings, which were consistent with balance of payments targets, with banks allocating foreign exchange to their client public enterprises. From 1991, the Council on Money and Credit was made responsible for setting foreign exchange and external debt policy, and for approving foreign investments and joint ventures. The Supplementary Finance Law of August 1990 granted businesses and individuals the right to hold foreign currency ac-

---

[42]Except for private vehicles until the end of 1994.

[43]Goods banned for religious, health, or social reasons; goods temporarily suspended until the end of 1994; and 10 basic commodities—mostly subsidized food staples—whose restrictions were phased out by the end of 1994.

counts. Between 1989 and 1991, the Algerian dinar was allowed to depreciate to counteract the terms of trade losses during this period. In 1991, as part of an attempt to realign domestic relative prices and increase openness, the Algerian dinar was devalued by more than 100 percent to DA 22 per U.S. dollar (see Figure 15). During 1991–94, the rate of nominal depreciation averaged only 4 percent annually, bringing the value of the Algerian dinar to about DA 24 per U.S. dollar on the official market. This relative stability of the nominal rate did not correspond to economic fundamentals: adverse terms of trade shocks and expansionary domestic financial policies had led to inflation persistently higher than Algeria's trading partners. The Algerian dinar, therefore, appreciated by 50 percent in real terms between October 1991 and the end of 1993, while the ratio between the parallel market rate and the official rate—which had fallen from about 5 in the mid-1980s to 2 in 1991—rose again to 4 by early 1994.

The immediate objectives at the outset of the adjustment program in 1994 were to correct the overvaluation of the Algerian dinar, allowing its value to be determined by market forces, and to make the system more transparent. A large devaluation of the Algerian dinar of about 50 percent took place in two steps: in March–April 1994, bringing the Algerian dinar to DA 36 per U.S. dollar; then again at the end of September 1994, bringing the Algerian dinar to DA 41 per U.S. dollar. The parallel rate fell to about twice the official rate during this time.

Following the devaluation in 1994, the exchange rate was managed flexibly, and some nominal depreciation took place until mid-1996 (Figure 15). Since that time, tight financial policies and the strengthening in Algeria's external position have resulted in increased nominal exchange rate stability, helping in turn to anchor lower inflationary expectations. The authorities intend to continue allowing market forces to determine the exchange rate, while adapting their intervention to avoid any sustained real effective appreciation, thus promoting economic diversification. Such a policy would help protect Algeria from some of the destabilizing effects of energy price volatility by facilitating adjustment in the face of external shocks. A deepening in the domestic financial and foreign exchange markets and their integration into global financial markets would further enhance this process.

Reform of the Exchange System

In the 1970s and 1980s, the central bank allocated foreign exchange, mostly from hydrocarbon exports, by a centralized system of import licenses awarded to approved trading entities. In addition to a complicated system of import authorizations, Algeria maintained a set of exchange premiums for remittances in

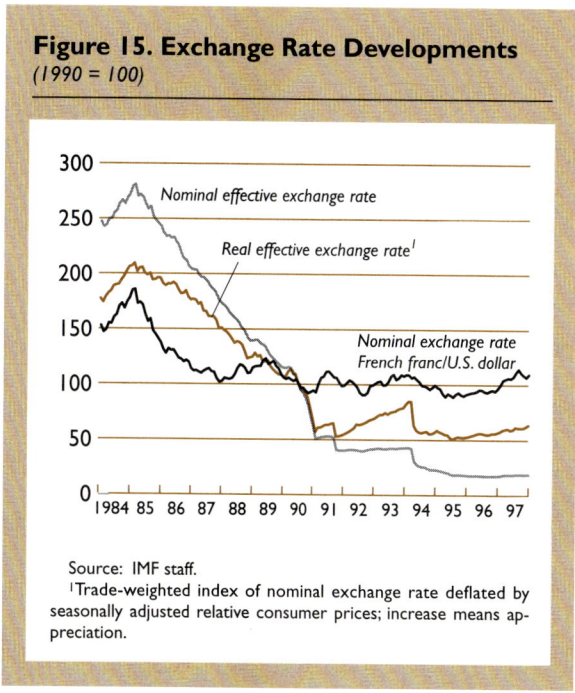

Figure 15. Exchange Rate Developments
(1990 = 100)

Source: IMF staff.
[1]Trade-weighted index of nominal exchange rate deflated by seasonally adjusted relative consumer prices; increase means appreciation.

excess of preset thresholds that constituted multiple currency practices. On the export side, exporters—with few exceptions—were generally not allowed to retain export earnings, and allowances for travel abroad were restricted. Under the two IMF arrangements between 1989 and 1992, currency convertibility was seen as key for greater economic efficiency and sustained growth. Financial imbalances coupled with high debt-service payments, however, led to a tightening of restrictions on international transactions in 1992–93: minimum maturities for new trade credits were enforced, while access to foreign exchange or credits was increasingly denied to importers. The immediate concern of the authorities was to lower the debt-service ratio and avoid resorting to a debt rescheduling.

Beginning in October 1994, the exchange rate became flexible by means of daily fixing sessions, organized by the Bank of Algeria. The exchange rate for all transactions was determined daily based on bids submitted by commercial banks at the beginning of each session and the availability of foreign exchange. An important step taken in January 1996 was the introduction of an interbank foreign exchange market in which commercial banks and financial institutions were allowed to hold positions in foreign currencies and trade among themselves. Foreign exchange surrender requirements for exports were lowered on average and unified at 50 percent, with the exception of earnings from hydrocarbon and mining exports. Export proceeds could be repa-

VII EXTERNAL SECTOR DEVELOPMENTS

triated directly on the interbank foreign exchange market and represented, in the initial stage, the bulk of resources for banks and financial institutions.

As oil export proceeds from Sonatrach revert to the Bank of Algeria, the latter remains the largest supplier of foreign exchange, and hence plays a major role in the interbank market. Nonetheless, commercial banks have adapted well to the new system and to new prudential regulations on open foreign positions established with IMF assistance. The system of foreign currency accounts was retained at this stage to preserve confidence among foreign exchange earners, particularly the private sector, and to avoid disrupting workers' remittances. A further step in the exchange system reform, the establishment of *bureaux de change* to deepen the market and broaden the public's access to foreign exchange, took place in December 1996.

Payments for current transactions were also liberalized. In April 1994, the Comité Ad Hoc was dissolved; the rule that some imports be exclusively financed by the importer's own resources was eliminated; and minimum maturity requirements on import financing were abolished, with the exception of capital goods imports, which were gradually phased out in 1995. By mid-1995, all exchange rate controls on merchandise trade were dismantled. Restrictions on payments for invisibles were to be removed in stages—first for health and education, and later for all other invisibles. In addition, banks became free to provide foreign exchange to importers for bona fide requests, while the Bank of Algeria ended the provision of forward cover on foreign exchange that had been extended to enterprises. The system of foreign currency accounts, however, was retained to promote confidence among foreign exchange earners and attract foreign remittances. By the end of 1996, payments for health, education, and other expenditures abroad could also be authorized by commercial banks up to a specific ceiling beyond which Bank of Algeria authorization was required. The final restrictions on payments for the remaining current transactions, including tourism travel, were lifted in 1997, and Algeria accepted the obligations of Article VIII in September 1997.

External Debt Burden and Critical Role of External Financing

Algeria borrowed heavily in the 1980s and much of this borrowing was used to finance either consumption or investments with low rates of return in the ailing state industrial complex. As a result, the stock of medium- and long-term external debt rose to 70 percent of GDP in 1994, while its average maturity had fallen substantially since much of the new borrowing in the early 1990s took the form of short-term suppliers' credits maturing in one to three years. Consequently, annual debt service costs rose to more than $9 billion, equivalent to 82 percent of total export receipts and almost one-fourth of GDP. In conjuction with the 1991 Stand-By Arrangement, the Algerian authorities eschewed a comprehensive debt rescheduling in favor of voluntary refinancings on a creditor-by-creditor basis reprofilage. These reschedulings only dealt with a small part of the external debt on a voluntary basis and did not provide sufficient relief.[44] Nevertheless, the government continued to scrupulously meet all external debt payments until they reached 85 percent of export proceeds. The external payments situation then became unsustainable and, in April 1994, Algeria requested a comprehensive debt rescheduling from its bilateral official and commercial creditors.

With the request for multilateral debt rescheduling, capital inflows declined markedly, mostly because official export credit agencies withdrew cover to Algeria. Paradoxically external borrowing, which had consistently exceeded $6 billion annually in the late 1980s and early 1990s—when macroeconomic imbalances were rising—dropped to $4.5 billion in 1994, $3.2 billion in 1995, and further to $1.7 billion in 1997, when macroeconomic stability was restored. Offsetting this decline, however, Algeria received balance of payments support of more than $21 billion between 1994 and March 1998, most of which came from debt rescheduling by the Paris and London Clubs (see Box 12). The remainder was provided as balance of payments support by multilateral financial institutions, most notably the IMF, which provided about $3 billion during this period. Overall, the combination of exceptional financing and new borrowing from official and commercial creditors provided Algeria with external financing of about $30 billion between 1994 and 1997: $10.3 billion in 1994, $9.3 billion in 1995, $6.3 billion in 1996, and $4.7 billion in 1997.

External financing aided the adjustment process in Algeria through several channels. First, in the absence of balance of payments support during the initial stages, growth, investment, and consumption would have undergone a much more severe and prolonged slump than actually occurred. After experiencing declines in 1993–94, real GDP grew by more than 4 percent in 1995 and 1996, the highest consecutive rates of economic growth since 1985. Without this financing, ceteris paribus, imports would have been lower, thereby jeopardizing growth prospects by reducing

---

[44]A rescheduling of debts, amounting to $2.3 billion, was conducted in May 1991 with the Italian Export Credit Insurance Agency (SACE), and in March 1992, $1.5 billion was rescheduled with a group of commercial banks headed by the Credit Lyonnais.

Future Prospects

> ## Box 12. Rescheduling with the Paris and London Clubs
>
> **Paris Club**
>
> In *June 1994*, following the approval of a Stand-By Arrangement with the IMF, Algeria agreed on a debt rescheduling package with the Paris Club group of official bilateral creditors. Algeria obtained relatively generous rescheduling terms, with creditors agreeing to include debts contracted before September 1993—the "cutoff date"—and a graduated repayment schedule over 15 years with a short grace period (compared with the standard Paris Club terms of 10 years' maturity with five years' grace). The rescheduling covered loans with an original maturity of over one year extended to, or guaranteed by, the government of Algeria (including state agencies), and excluded creditors with claims of less than SDR 1 million falling due during the consolidation period (although these were to be paid on the original due dates or no later than a specified deadline).[1] The 1994 agreement contained a so-called "goodwill clause," indicating that Paris Club creditor members would meet in principle to consider pre-cutoff debts falling due after May 31, 1995, provided Algeria implemented the terms of the agreement, continued to have a program with the IMF, and reached refinancing arrangements with other creditors on comparable terms.
>
> In *July 1995*, after the approval of the Extended Arrangement with the IMF in May 1995, a follow-up "exit" rescheduling was agreed. Given the short maturities on Algeria's debt, the second rescheduling effectively amounted to a restructuring of most of Algeria's debt stock.[2] Indeed, in 1995, Algeria received debt relief on principal falling due over a span of three years (the consolidation period) as compared to the standard Paris Club consolidation period of 12 months to 18 months (as received in 1994). The agreement stipulated that the provisions would apply each year until 1998, provided Algeria continues to have an arrangement in good standing with the IMF (to be confirmed by IMF reports to the Paris Club), and that Algeria has made on due dates all payments referred to in the agreement to Paris Club creditors. In late 1996, the Paris Club implemented the second tranche of the agreement, covering maturities through June 1997, and the implementation of the third tranche was approved in July 1997.
>
> The Paris Club deals provided over $12 billion in cashflow relief during the period covered by the Stand-By and Extended Arrangements. This had a significant impact on Algeria's debt-service costs, which fell from 82 percent of exports in 1993 to 42 percent in 1995, and an estimated 31 percent in 1996.
>
> **London Club**
>
> Algeria reached an agreement in *September 1995* with the Steering Committee of Commercial Banks—known as the London Club—on the terms of commercial debt rescheduling that was endorsed by all participants in June 1996. The agreement covered debts falling due between March 1, 1994 and December 31, 1997: a total of $3.23 billion, including $1 billion in previously rescheduled debt. Under this agreement, all previously rescheduled debts (excluding those owed to Japanese leasing companies) were rescheduled over 15½ years, with a 6½ years' grace period. This new amortization period is longer not only than the one granted by commercial banks on previously rescheduled debts, but also than the one granted by Paris Club creditors on pre-cutoff date debt. The London Club agreement also included provisions for debt/equity conversions, debt buybacks, and debt exchanges.
>
> ---
>
> [1]Specifically, the June 1994 agreement rescheduled the following pre-cutoff date obligations: (1) all principal and interest due and not paid as of May 31, 1994; (2) all principal falling due between June 1, 1994 and May 31, 1995; and (3) all interest falling due between June 1, 1994 and October 31, 1994. Rescheduled amounts were to be repaid in 24 semiannual, gradually increasing installments starting on May 31, 1998.
>
> [2]The July 1995 agreement rescheduled pre-cutoff date obligations for (1) all principal falling due between June 1, 1995 and May 31, 1998; and (2) all interest falling due between June 1, 1995 and May 31, 1996. The provisions of the June 1994 agreement were not affected by the 1995 deal. Repayments on these amounts are to be made in 25 semiannual gradually increasing installments starting on November 30, 1999 and ending in 2011.

imports of capital goods and intermediate inputs. In 1995, imports of investment goods and consumer durables recovered strongly as pent-up demand was unleashed by the trade liberalization of 1994–95. In a climate of economic austerity, eliminating shortages and filling stores with foodstuffs and consumer products—albeit at high prices—may have had an important positive influence on public support for the program. Second, it allowed Algeria to restore reserves from an uncomfortably low level in 1993 to almost three months of imports in 1994, thereby providing an important signal of stability to international markets. With higher oil prices, official foreign exchange reserves reached the equivalent of almost nine months of imports by the end of 1997, and debt service as a share of total export receipts fell to 30 percent.

Future Prospects

To date, even in the absence of large capital flows outside the oil sector, Algeria's balance of payments

VII External Sector Developments

position has strengthened dramatically—owing to the tight domestic demand policies and a recovery in oil prices. Resort to exceptional balance of payments financing is expected to cease in 1998. While still high, debt and debt-service ratios are expected to fall to below 30 percent in the medium term, even on the basis of fairly conservative oil prices. With the improvement in Algeria's financial position and the restoration of macroeconomic balances, international confidence has resumed—as illustrated by the increase in the secondary market price of Algerian debt from $0.56 in September 1996 to about $0.88 by June 1998—and Algeria's access to external financing has begun to recover.

Algeria's balance of payments position, however, remains fragile and sensitive to a number of elements beyond its control, particularly the vagaries of international oil prices. Fluctuations in oil prices have obvious implications for the trade balance since hydrocarbon exports continue to represent about 95 percent of total export receipts.[45] Notwithstanding the need for reducing the country's vulnerability by diversifying exports, hydrocarbon exports are likely to continue to dominate Algeria's trade flows in the long term in view of the country's proven hydrocarbon reserves, particularly natural gas. Moreover, aside from the impact of the hydrocarbon sector on the domestic economy, other elements of the balance of payments are affected by growth prospects in the industry, such as trade in oil-related services, and foreign investment and related imports.

In addition, Algeria continues to be vulnerable to changes in world cereal prices, since it is the largest importer of durum wheat. Its total food imports exceed $2 billion. There is substantial scope for reducing this vulnerability, as price liberalization in agriculture has increased production, while granting property rights to farmers in 1998 is expected to lead to an increase in investment.

A third key element for future sustainable growth compatible with external viability will be Algeria's ability to attract non-debt-creating private capital flows, especially for investment in the nonhydrocarbon sector. The external debt burden is still high, and new external borrowing is likely to be undertaken prudently. As the economy evolves and market forces are free to allocate resources to their most productive uses, Algeria should be able to attract capital flows and direct investment commensurate with the economy's productive potential. This would permit higher imports and promote the acquisition of foreign technology and expertise. Improved confidence in Algeria's economic prospects and a stabilization of the economic and political picture will be instrumental in Algeria's ability to attract higher levels of foreign investment.

---

[45]Since the 1980s, in an attempt to cushion the impact of oil price changes, Algeria has strived to diversify its hydrocarbon sector and has successfully expanded the production of natural gas and crude oil derivatives to the extent that, by 1996, crude oil exports amounted to only 24.6 percent of total hydrocarbon export revenues, while natural gas exports accounted for 33.9 percent, with the remainder being petroleum products.

VIII Achievements and Future Challenges

For about twenty-five years following its independence in 1962, Algeria made significant progress toward developing its human and physical infrastructure, as well as a vigorous and diversified hydrocarbon sector. Income and gender inequalities were reduced, and a large degree of social cohesion was attained. The yearly flow of the petroleum rent and trade protection, however, shielded the Algerian economy from the inefficiencies inherent in its central planning of resources and in the one-party political system. Large investments in industrial development did little to create a diversified and competitive industrial base, while neglecting pressing housing needs, which reached crisis proportion.

The hydrocarbon shield was shattered with the reverse oil shock in 1986 and again in 1988, which coincided with the first political demonstrations that hit Algeria's cities. It then became clear to policymakers that Algeria could no longer sustain an inward-oriented command economy, which subsidized its public enterprises and remained fully dependent on oil revenues. A gradual process of liberalization and reform was launched, reorienting the institutional framework toward one more compatible with a market economy. In particular, agricultural production and land tenure were increasingly liberalized, and greater autonomy was given to public enterprises.

This process gathered some momentum with IMF- and Bank-supported reform programs in both 1989 and 1991. Nevertheless, throughout this period, reform lacked a comprehensive vision and was mostly reactive to pressure points. As a result, liberalization in some areas coincided with a tightening of restrictions in other areas, exacerbating distortions and generating shortages of both imports and domestic goods and services. Above all, these reforms lacked the political will to make a decisive break with past reliance on government as the major provider of employment, housing, food subsidies, and financing for public enterprises. They neither had the demand management underpinnings nor a broad measure of support by labor unions and managers in both the private and public sectors. Attempts at easing shortages with short-term external financing of imports only bloated external debt and precipitated a payments crisis at the end of 1993. Rising unemployment, an acute housing shortage, and growing civil strife added further gloom to Algeria's economic prospects.

The reform program launched in April 1994, in a difficult social and political environment, marked a new beginning as well as a new consensual approach. Indeed, after the failure in attempting to develop market mechanisms while maintaining a massive presence of the state in the economy, policymakers came to acknowledge that a change of strategy was needed. There was a fundamental recognition that for Algeria to be able to address its acute social and political problems, it had to reinvigorate its economy and ensure high and sustained growth, but that this objective could only be achieved by abandoning central planning and establishing an outward-oriented and efficient market economy, conducive to private sector activity and integrated with the rest of the world. This recognition provided a unifying approach to the transition and reform process, which was well sequenced and comprehensive. The initial emphasis was to set the exchange rate at a more realistic level, realign relative prices, eliminate distortions through liberalization, and stabilize domestic demand. At the same time, the following structural reforms, to be implemented over two to three years, were set in motion: public enterprise reform and privatization, banking system restructuring, social safety net provisions, and the establishment of market mechanisms such as the use of indirect instruments of monetary policy and the creation of interbank markets for foreign exchange and bank refinancing.

Within three years, by the end of 1997, this reform program had achieved remarkable success in restoring financial stability and establishing the building blocks for a market economy. While Algeria has been a latecomer in the reform process relative to other countries in the region, it has adjusted faster (see Box 13 and Figure 16).

- Inflation declined to 6 percent, and after a decade of declining per capita income, there were three consecutive years of positive growth in 1995, 1996, and 1997.

VIII ACHIEVEMENTS AND FUTURE CHALLENGES

> **Box 13. Catching Up with Reformers**
>
> A number of countries in the MENA region, Morocco, Tunisia, Jordan, and Egypt, have successfully undertaken macroeconomic stabilization and wide-ranging structural reforms under IMF-supported programs. Morocco and Tunisia started comparatively early and have gone furthest: Morocco's adjustment efforts since 1980 were supported by nine IMF arrangements, with an arrangement in effect at least part of every year during 1980–93, while Tunisia entered in 1986 a Stand-By Arrangement, followed subsequently by a four-year Extended Fund Facility. Both countries have by now successfully graduated from IMF programs. Jordan and Egypt were threatened by growing financial imbalances in the late 1980s, but Jordan's initial adjustment efforts were hindered by the crisis in 1990–91, and comprehensive reforms were launched in earnest with a Stand-By Arrangement in 1992. Jordan then entered into Extended Fund Facility programs in 1994 and 1996, the latter ending in February 1999. Egypt initiated a stabilization program in 1991, whereas structural reforms accelerated in the mid-1990s, particularly in the context of the current two-year precautionary Stand-By Arrangement, which runs until October 1998.
>
> While the experience of each of these countries is necessarily unique, a common thread runs through all of them. In the face of external shocks, they all attempted to maintain high absorption levels, giving rise to large budget deficits—generally monetized—widening current account deficits, overvalued exchange rates, growing external debt, and eventually debt-servicing difficulties that precipitated adjustment. The stabilization and structural reforms adopted to redress the situation received substantial financial support from the IMF and the international community, including through debt reschedulings and, in some cases, relief. In the event, all these countries have proved successful in sharply reducing budget and current account deficits, bringing down inflation to single-digit levels, going a long way toward restoring sustained economic growth, and achieving external viability, with comfortable levels of foreign exchange reserves, declining external debt burdens, and a resumption of capital inflows.
>
> Major progress has also been registered on the structural front, with price, trade, and exchange liberalization; tax, financial sector, and legal reforms; and the restructuring and privatization of large and inefficient public enterprises.
>
> Algeria's successful experience resembles in many ways that of the other MENA reformers, but a number of features set it apart. First, whereas Algeria embarked on its program comparatively later, in mid-1994, it has adjusted faster (Figure 16). By the end of 1996, Algeria's macroeconomic performance equaled or even surpassed that of the early starters: real growth was 4 percent; inflation was declining to single-digits, both the budget and the current account posted surpluses; foreign reserves were at five months of imports; and external debt indicators had improved markedly. Second, oil plays a more predominant role: while the reverse oil shocks contributed to trigger the crisis, since then, Algeria has succeeded in diversifying its hydrocarbon sector and expanding gas exports, boosted by new discoveries, but oil prices remain crucial. Third, the legacy of central planning was heavier than in the other countries, and hence more radical structural changes are needed to allow market forces to play. Finally, reforms have faced the additional hurdle of having to be carried out against a background of civil strife.
>
> Looking ahead, all these countries face largely similar challenges, though to a varying degree: to consolidate macroeconomic stabilization, to step up and deepen structural reforms, and to promote further integration with the world economy, so as to foster competitiveness and growth, while protecting the most vulnerable. Algeria's task is nonetheless complicated by its own particular set of fragilities: high unemployment and a rapidly growing labor force that could only be absorbed through high growth rates in the nonhydrocarbon sector (see Figure 17); the vulnerability to fluctuations in international oil prices and dependence on food imports; its still heavy external debt burden; a fledgling private sector; and the need for institutional reforms and a political environment that would be conducive to private domestic and foreign investment.

- A market-oriented price system was established, eliminating price restrictions and generalized subsidies.
- A surplus was achieved in the fiscal and external accounts (even when allowance is made for the increase in oil prices), with a substantial buildup of external reserves to seven months of imports by the end of 1997, and a reduction in the external debt service ratio from 83 percent in 1993 to 30 percent in 1997.
- The government's disengagement from production and trading activities was accompanied by the establishment of a market-oriented banking system that imposed a tight budget constraint on its clients, including public enterprises (see Box 14).

In addition to the above-mentioned strong political will, several elements account for the successful implementation of the program.

- The savings realized from the elimination of generalized food subsidies allowed the funding of a more efficient social safety net with a job-creation program, unemployment insurance, and cash transfers to the most disadvantaged groups. Budgetary appropriations for public housing were

Achievements and Future Challenges

Box 14. Reducing the Size of the Public Sector in the Economy

Background

- Reducing the share of the public sector in the economy constitutes a major pillar of the government's strategy to allow the emergence of a dynamic private sector. Much has been accomplished in the last few years. In 1991, more than one-half of the labor force worked for the public sector (about 70 percent of industry, more than one-half of construction, and 30 percent of services, while agriculture was dominated by small private farms). Most public companies were operating with obsolete technologies and antiquated management under central planning, resulting in lack of competition, which, coupled with a high degree of protection, distorted resource allocation. Moreover, these fragilities were exacerbated by the liberalization process, which led rapidly to mounting losses and created an unsustainable burden on the financial system.

- In the early stages of the transition to the market, the authorities favored a comprehensive restructuring of public enterprises, with a view to ensuring financial viability of public enterprises before moving toward privatization. During 1991–96, legal and financial autonomy was progressively granted to all public enterprises, accompanied by a program of financial rehabilitation, mainly through debt forgiveness from the treasury and swaps of government bonds for nonperforming debts to commercial banks and the housing bank. Debt conversion operations amounted to DA 357 billion in 1991–96 (4 percent of 1991–96 GDP), with DA 187 billion (6.8 percent of GDP) devoted in 1997 to cleaning up the balance sheet of food importing agencies, SNTF and Sonelgaz. In addition, public enterprises received DA 110 billion over 1991–96 (1.3 percent of GDP) in cash transfers through the Rehabilitation Fund established in 1991. The Rehabilitation Fund was terminated in December 1996.

Progress to Date

- A first privatization program was launched with the support of the World Bank in April 1996; it included the enactment of a privatization law. The program focused mainly on the 1,300 local public enterprises (EPL). Of the 274 EPL covered, 117 had been privatized or liquidated by the end of 1996. After a relatively slow start, privatization gained momentum with the creation of five regional holdings in charge of implementing the divestment operation. By April 1998, 827 EPLs had already been liquidated and 50 more are currently being sold. Most of these liquidations have resulted in important layoffs. However, 464 EPLs have been sold to their employees resulting in the creation of 608 new companies, protecting 12,141 jobs. The authorities have announced that by the end of 1998, the privatization process of the EPLs would be almost completed, culminating in the closure of most regional holdings.

- Considerable progress has been reached regarding the "offices" or food-importing and distributing agencies. At the end of October 1996, seven of the 10 agencies launched restructuring plans, conditional on performance contracts, and the other three (ENIAL, ENAFLA, and ONAPSA) were dissolved. In 1997, ENAPAL, which was responsible for importing most foodstuff until 1994, was dissolved, spelling the end of the state involvement in those activities. Moreover, the 18 units of the three dairy agencies were converted into subsidiaries to facilitate their privatization. In addition, the three pharmaceutical companies were recapitalized, all without exceeding the ceiling of DA 143 billion earmarked for the buyback of the agencies' debts. In early 1998, the large network of 1,139 pharmacies started to be sold.

- As for the more than 400 large public companies (EPEs), massive financial resources were used in an attempt to keep public industry functioning. At the same time, financial autonomy was granted to most EPEs to create incentives to reduce losses and limit the burden on the budget. However, little was achieved in terms of tackling in depth the restructuring needs or privatizing these enterprises, with the exception of the construction sector, where increasing difficulties led to substantial labor shedding. Nonetheless, some acceleration in the restructuring process was registered in late 1996. After grouping EPEs in 11 sectoral holdings, a bank-enterprise mechanism that imposed hard budget constraints was set up. As a result, by December 1997, 76 EPEs had been dissolved and almost 160,000 workers had been dismissed (about 30 percent of the total number of employees at the end of 1996). At the same time, in December 1997, the government announced a list of 250 EPEs to be privatized (about 30 percent of the remaining EPEs in terms of labor and turnover). The authorities are confident that some major privatizations can take place by the end of 1998. As of now, the EPEs on the list of privatizable enterprises in the chemical and mechanical engineering sectors are being evaluated by international consultants to enhance transparency of the privatization process.

raised. The social components of the program were essential in gaining workers' union support.

- Both demand management and structural reforms were steadfastly implemented. Despite the succession of three prime ministers during this period, persistent civil strife, declining real wages, and large layoffs stemming from public enterprise restructuring, there was no weakening in public policy or wavering in the public commitment to reform. Continuity was maintained by an independent central bank, and follow up was exercised by a standing ministerial committee chaired by the Prime Minister with the sole

VIII ACHIEVEMENTS AND FUTURE CHALLENGES

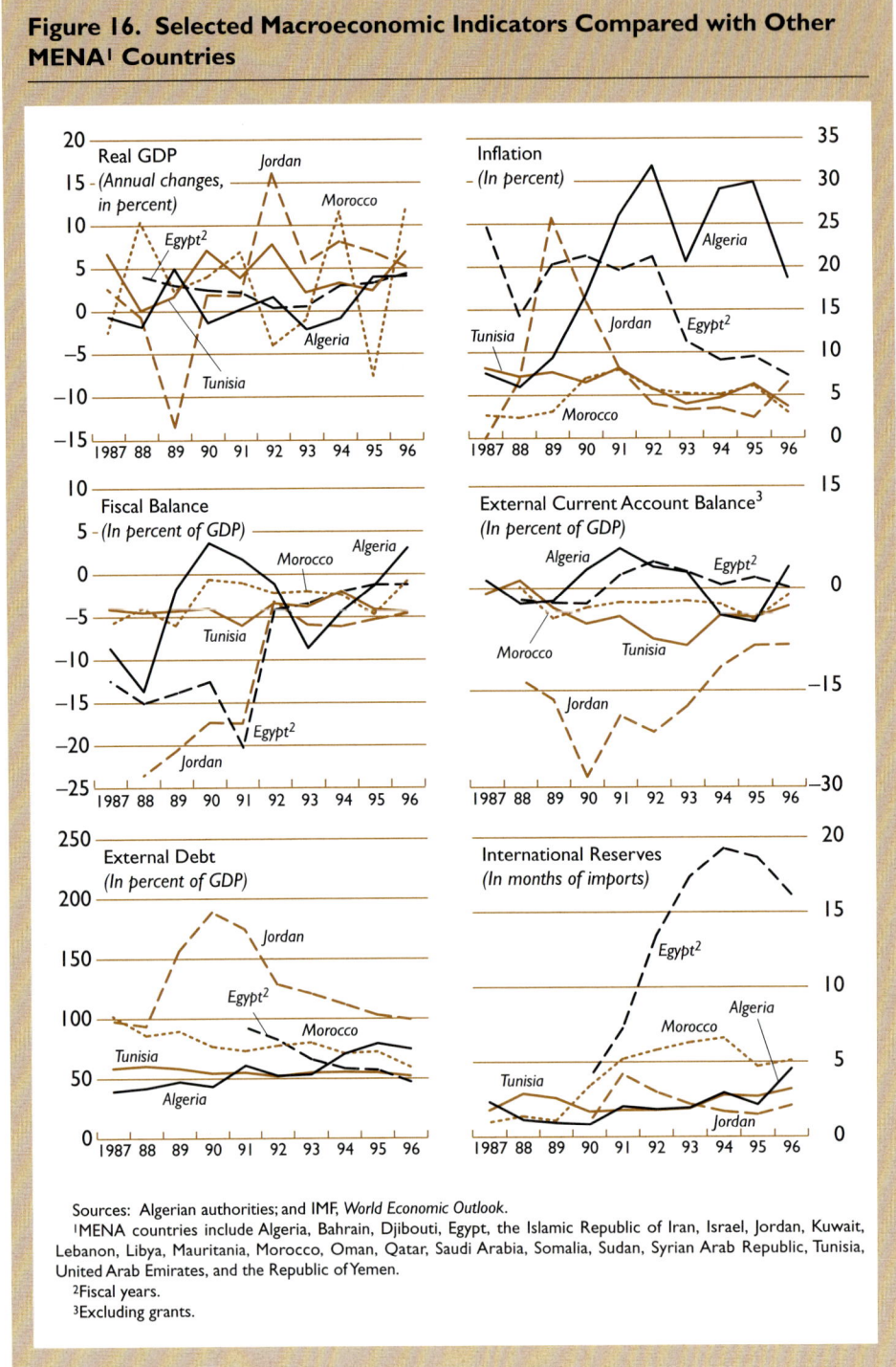

Figure 16. Selected Macroeconomic Indicators Compared with Other MENA¹ Countries

Sources: Algerian authorities; and IMF, *World Economic Outlook*.
¹MENA countries include Algeria, Bahrain, Djibouti, Egypt, the Islamic Republic of Iran, Israel, Jordan, Kuwait, Lebanon, Libya, Mauritania, Morocco, Oman, Qatar, Saudi Arabia, Somalia, Sudan, Syrian Arab Republic, Tunisia, United Arab Emirates, and the Republic of Yemen.
²Fiscal years.
³Excluding grants.

responsibility of implementing the reform program. This whole process was supported by a dedicated civil service that ensured smooth policy coordination among the central bank, the ministry of finance, and other ministries and government agencies. Consequently, when slippages in credit policy occurred in the summer of 1995, corrective action was quickly taken.

- A flexible exchange rate policy was pursued, which in Algeria's case also played an important demand management role because of the large oil revenues that accrue to the budget. While the reduction in inflation may have taken longer, price competitiveness was preserved. Authorities successfully reduced inflation through strict demand management policies. As these policies firmly took hold in the budget and in wage negotiations, the exchange rate depreciation of the first two years gave way to a substantial degree of price stability in 1996 and 1997.

- When oil prices increased sharply in 1996 and 1997, most of the oil windfall was saved. This reserve has helped cushion the recent oil price decline and will considerably ease repayment of rescheduled external debt beginning in 2000.
- Comprehensive structural reforms with excellent coordination between the IMF, the World Bank, and the Algerian authorities took place. While the IMF concentrated its assistance on macroeconomic stabilization, liberalization of prices and trade and the social safety net, the World Bank assisted in the restructuring of public enterprises, the audit and financial restructuring of banks, housing, and privatization. Without public enterprise and bank reform, neither macrostabilization nor liberalization could be sustained. All these aspects must be tackled simultaneously.
- A broad consensus for reform through periodic negotiations among the government, management (of both public and private enterprises), and labor unions was established. Commitments under World Bank and IMF programs were made public and widely debated in the press, establishing Algeria's full ownership of the reform program.
- An appropriate sequencing of measures took account of the public's concerns. While some prices were quickly liberalized, food and energy subsidies were phased out gradually over three years through gradual price increases. Private sector importers were phased in into sensitive areas, such as pharmaceuticals and essential food staples, hitherto monopolized by the public sector.
- Algeria benefited from large financial assistance from foreign donors and international institutions. About $22 billion was provided over a three-year period ($17 billion in debt rescheduling and $5 billion in new lending from international and regional institutions) to support external trade and payment liberalization, eliminate import shortages, and sustain per capita consumption. This infusion of external support eased the burden of adjustment considerably and restored the sustainability to Algeria's external debt profile.

While Algeria made remarkable progress in macroeconomic stabilization and in establishing market mechanisms, other structural reforms proved more difficult to implement and, in some cases, more intractable.

The legacy of past government intervention in prices and external trade resulted in a string of quasi-fiscal deficits, which were financed by the banking system and could not be identified early on in the program. For instance, government food importing agencies could not service their external debt—which had more than doubled after the devaluation—from current operations, but had to rely on domestic or external bank financing. When such financing was sharply reduced in the context of stricter bank lending policies, these agencies defaulted and their bank loans were taken over by the treasury. A lesson for future IMF programs is to fully flesh out the external debt implications on the financial condition of banks and enterprises following a large devaluation.

The housing crisis proved difficult to address despite the best efforts of the authorities, the World Bank, and the IMF. This was partly due to the need to restructure the entire system of housing construction and financing, while ensuring a steady yearly delivery rate. The latter was essential to ease existing shortages and provide jobs. With the benefit of hindsight, greater progress would have required a high-level task force endowed with broad powers that superseded individual ministries to obtain and develop construction sites and to mobilize financing. The establishment of clear property rights in agriculture and in housing also proved elusive, which is understandable given 30 years of socialist legacy. The absence of such rights inhibits collateralization of bank financing, reduces incentives for investment, and limits bank intermediation. Indeed, the judicial system in Algeria is not yet geared to the norms of a market economy. It is slow and cumbersome in contractual disputes, and favors tenants over landlords.

Foreign direct investment outside the hydrocarbon sector, which is essential for modernizing the capital stock and for injecting best management practices, as well as domestic private sector investment have not been forthcoming to the extent anticipated. They have been inhibited by the civil strife which, in addition to the psychological impact, has exacted substantial costs. These costs include lost production, mostly in agriculture and industry; damage to infrastructure; costs associated with the provision of security services; higher transportation costs; cost of relocating plants to safer areas; and costs of uncollected taxes and rents in areas that lack security. It has also reduced labor mobility.

Future Challenges

It should be recalled that the major objectives of Algeria's economic reform strategy were to secure

VIII ACHIEVEMENTS AND FUTURE CHALLENGES

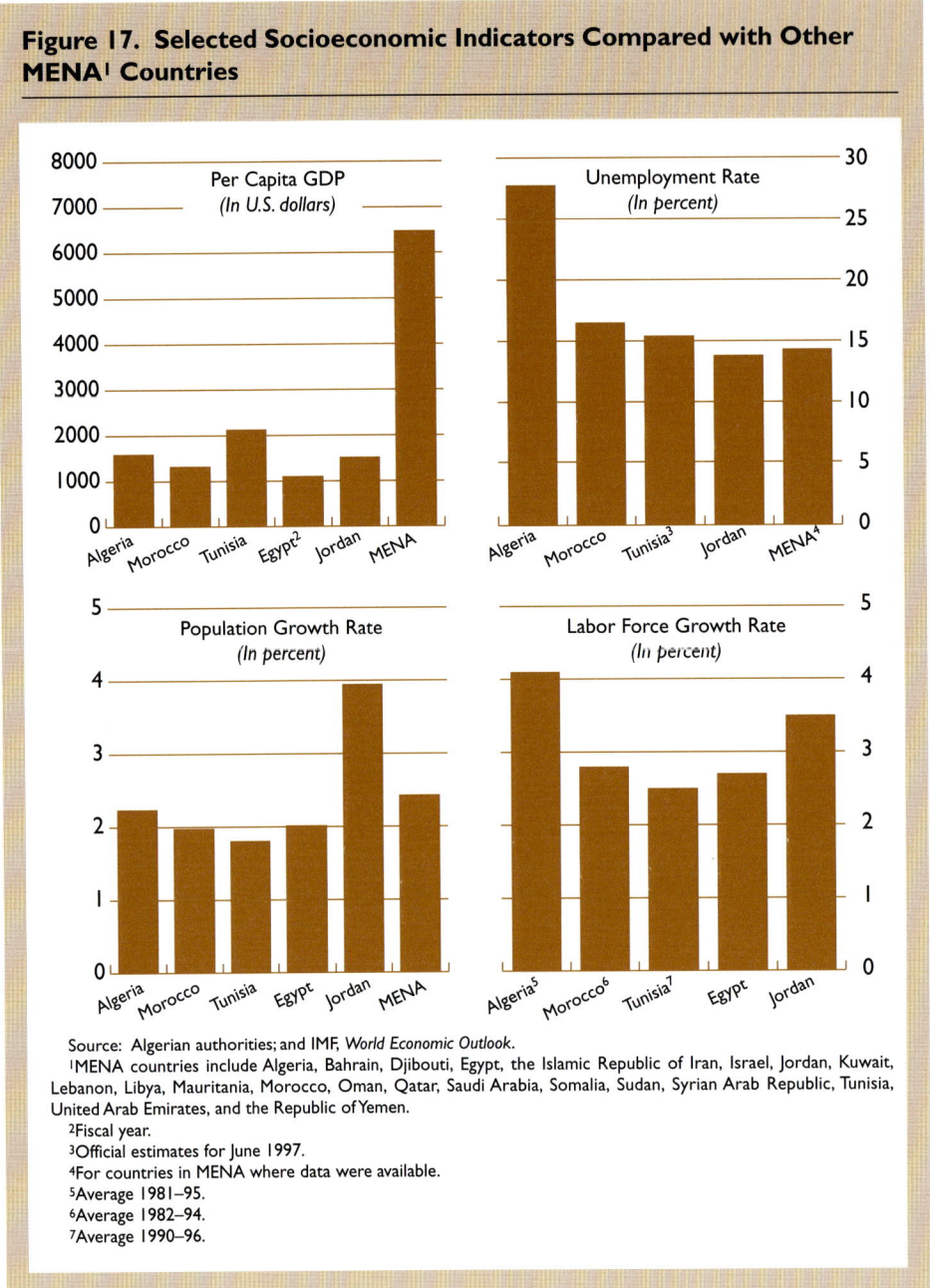

Figure 17. Selected Socioeconomic Indicators Compared with Other MENA[1] Countries

Source: Algerian authorities; and IMF, *World Economic Outlook*.
[1]MENA countries include Algeria, Bahrain, Djibouti, Egypt, the Islamic Republic of Iran, Israel, Jordan, Kuwait, Lebanon, Libya, Mauritania, Morocco, Oman, Qatar, Saudi Arabia, Somalia, Sudan, Syrian Arab Republic, Tunisia, United Arab Emirates, and the Republic of Yemen.
[2]Fiscal year.
[3]Official estimates for June 1997.
[4]For countries in MENA where data were available.
[5]Average 1981–95.
[6]Average 1982–94.
[7]Average 1990–96.

high sustainable growth and reduce unemployment. Considering that the labor force has been growing at almost 4 percent a year (a rising female participation is expected to offset the impact of a declining birth rate) and that industrial restructuring will entail some labor shedding, Algeria needs a yearly growth rate of 6 percent to 7 percent in the nonhydrocarbon sector, together with a concentration of growth in labor-intensive activities. These two conditions are necessary for a significant reduction in the 28 percent unemployment prevailing today (see Figure 17).

On a macroeconomic level, the major antilabor bias, arising from an overvalued exchange rate, negative real interest rates, and a state industrial policy that favored capital intensive industrial complexes over agriculture or housing, has been corrected. The exchange rate is realistic, real interest rates have become positive, and the government has started to withdraw from production activities. Other conditions, however, are necessary to ensure high and sustained growth that would reduce unemployment, maintain a high quality of public expenditure in the context of tight demand management, and ensure a diversification of the production base away from hydrocarbons. A flexible exchange rate policy and wage increases tied to productivity growth will be critical in this respect. In addition, much needs to be done at the micro level and in terms of structural reforms.

- The privatization of public enterprises is hindered by the small size of the private sector in Algeria and its lack of corporate structures and modern management practices. It is doubtful whether the private sector can absorb the large state-owned industries. Therefore, successful privatization would require a higher degree of public support for the program through a broadening of privatization mechanisms (e.g., vouchers, employee buy-outs, stock market listings, and so forth). The establishment of a stock market and adoption of standarized accounting practices with greater transparency would mobilize domestic savings and attract foreign partnerships and direct investment, which are essential to inject new technology and management.

- Modernization of the banking system with the help of foreign partnerships or privatization will be necessary to support a growing private sector and deepen financial intermediation. In this transitional environment, the reluctance of banks to assume risk has slowed down the private sector's efforts to take over some government activities and more generally to broaden their role in the economy. Consequently, there is a need to develop a banking culture and deepen financial markets, particularly for treasury bills and high quality commercial paper.

- Clear property rights in agriculture, housing, and urban real estate need to be established. Steps are being taken in the agricultural sector. In particular, a law was presented to parliament in mid-1998 to clarify land ownership.

- Housing delivery will have to be reoriented from the state to the private sector through the provision of financing and market incentives. This process has already been engaged and is being supplemented by the creation of a mortgage bank and other mechanisms, such as the creation of a secondary market in mortgages and a mortgage guarantee institution.

- The judicial system should be reformed to ensure a quick settlement of contractual disputes and bankruptcy proceedings. Civil courts need to be established in major cities. The regulatory framework also needs to be simplified and become transparent and more accessible to the public.

- Unemployment at 28 percent is high and a major cause of social instability. A concerted effort through labor market reforms, public investment in labor-intensive infrastructure, and the promotion of a competitive environment for private investment are essential to reduce unemployment and absorb new entrants to the labor force.

- The education system needs to be restructured to meet the labor profile required by the private sector and Algeria's economic integration in the Mediterranean basin.

- Algeria's integration into the world economy should be promoted by liberalizing further trade, services and capital flows, as well as fostering the absorption of new technologies, which will be essential to face the challenges posed by globalization.

Facing these challenges will not be easy, particularly if foreign investment continues to be deterred by security problems, but Algeria also holds great potential. Its dynamic hydrocarbon sector and considerable oil revenues provide both a large internal market and the government resources necessary to pursue the reforms outlined above. Its comparative advantage based on low labor costs and a capable human resource base as well as Algeria's proximity to the European markets and other Maghreb countries should provide large gains from trade. The recent broadening of political participation in government following the June and October 1997 elections offers the promise of progress in the restoration of peace. This, together with continued determination in completing the structural reforms outlined above, should contribute to create an enabling environment for a full realization of Algeria's potential.

Appendix I Algeria's Hydrocarbon Sector: Evolution and Prospects

The hydrocarbon sector dominates the Algerian economy. In 1997, it accounted for nearly 30 percent of GDP and contributed to 95 percent of export receipts and 60 percent of budgetary revenues. Because of the low labor intensity of production processes, the sector's share in aggregate employment is only about 3 percent.

According to the government of Algeria, proven recoverable reserves of crude oil were estimated at 9.98 billion barrels in 1996 and, at the current extraction rate, would be depleted in about 35 years (Organization of the Petroleum Exporting Countries (OPEC) estimates reserves at 9.2 billion barrels).[46] In addition, Algeria possesses enormous sedimentary basins that probably contain larger reserves of crude oil than current estimates suggest. Recoverable reserves will certainly rise in future years as a result of new discoveries and the installation of enhanced recovery systems. By contrast, proven natural gas reserves are more significant, amounting to 3,700 cubic meters (36 billion barrels of oil equivalent) at the beginning of 1996, and at current extraction rates would not be exhausted for at least 70 years.[47] In 1996, Algeria was the fourth largest natural gas exporter in the world. Algeria also has reserves of condensate and liquefied petroleum gas. According to the government, total recoverable hydrocarbon reserves in terms of tons of oil equivalent are broken down as follows: 57 percent for natural gas; 27 percent for crude; 9 percent for condensate; and 7 percent for liquefied petroleum gas.

The exploitation of hydrocarbon resources generates five different types of fuels, which are consumed domestically and/or exported: (1) crude oil, for which production is limited by Algeria's OPEC quota now set at 750,000 barrels a day; (2) refined petroleum products; (3) natural gas, which can be transported through pipelines or converted into liquefied natural gas; (4) condensate, which is a by-product of natural gas production; and (5) liquefied petroleum gas, which must be separated into butane and propane. The domestic market consumes about 20 percent of Algeria's total hydrocarbon sales (Figure 18).

Evolution of Hydrocarbon Strategy

Unlike most oil-producing countries, Algeria found itself with a well-diversified endowment of energy resources from the early 1950s. It was at that time that a French company, Entreprise de Recherches et d'Activités Pétrolières, discovered two giant oil and gas fields at Hassi-Messaoud and Hassi R'Mel, which still account for 70 percent of today's hydrocarbon output. This diversified endowment made the exploitation of gas products the potential centerpiece of Algeria's long-term hydrocarbon policy after independence in 1962, and the decision to exploit gas resources has helped to reduce the potential constraint

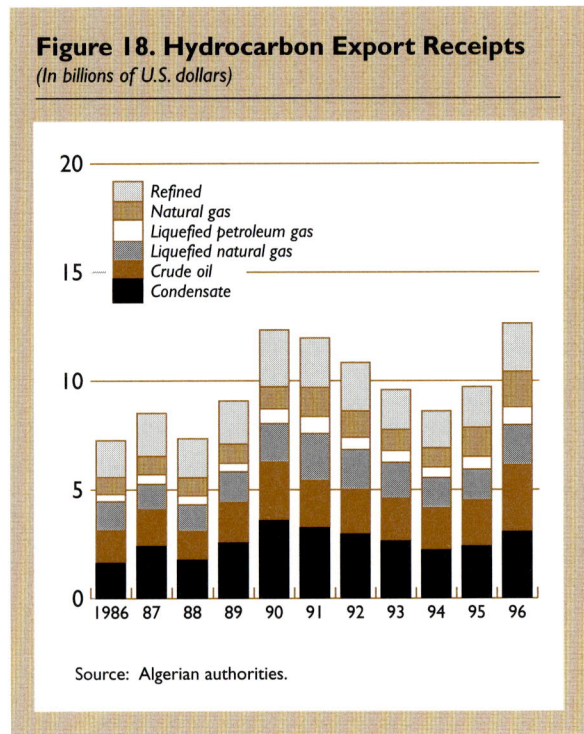

Figure 18. Hydrocarbon Export Receipts
(In billions of U.S. dollars)

Source: Algerian authorities.

---
[46]See Arab Petroleum Research Center, *Arab Oil and Gas Directory*, 1996.
[47]Ibid, 1994.

of OPEC quotas on crude oil imposed since the first oil shock in 1973. The subsequent oil price increases also made it profitable, first to undertake investments in gas liquefaction and liquefied natural gas transportation and, subsequently, to take advantage of its proximity to European markets through the construction of trans-Mediterranean pipelines. Thus, in the pursuit of a vision unique among oil producers, Algeria embarked on an ambitious—though not always successful—industrial and marketing strategy aimed at diversifying its hydrocarbon exports and establishing the country as a prime regional supplier of a broad menu of energy products.

Two phases can be identified in the evolution of this policy. From independence to the mid-1980s, the authorities emphasized economic nationalism in the context of a planned economy, which, ultimately, constrained production decisions and led to inefficient domestic pricing and suboptimal exploration efforts. In a second phase starting after the reverse oil shock in late 1986, the hydrocarbon sector was gradually opened to foreign participation while a more efficient domestic pricing policy was introduced. This strategy has improved oil recovery and gas export prospects.

Nationalistic Approach Under Central Planning

Following independence, the government's policy called for the transformation of the hydrocarbon sector into a highly integrated, state-owned complex under centralized management. Sonatrach,[48] the national oil company, was established in 1963 initially to transport and market hydrocarbons and, later, to carry out petroleum exploration, extraction, and processing. It became a quasi-monopoly in the early 1970s, following the nationalization of activities of foreign companies and the extension of state control over the whole hydrocarbon sector. By 1981, the state's share of the country's oil production had increased to 99 percent, from 77 percent in 1972, and 10 percent in 1962. The growing predominance of the state was established through Sonatrach's involvement in a wider range of downstream activities, including oil refining, and petrochemical production and marketing. Sonatrach also extended its purview to the development of pioneering gas liquefaction techniques.[49]

This industrial policy soon showed its limitations: economies from producing a wide range of products became quickly exhausted, and diseconomies in the management of this giant complex undermined its performance. In particular, oil and gas discoveries were hampered by the technological isolation in which Sonatrach had placed itself. Despite the vast, unprospected acreage available, the rate of discovery was just sufficient to prevent erosion of recoverable reserves and to stabilize the reserve-to-production ratio.[50] Partly because of this mixed performance, Sonatrach was restructured in 1982 and its mission restricted to upstream oil and gas activities and hydrocarbon exports. Several specialized state-owned enterprises were spun off from Sonatrach's divisions.[51] Yet, despite the industry's restructuring, Sonatrach and the other public enterprises of the hydrocarbon sector remained sheltered from external competition and unable to undertake cooperative ventures with foreign partners. This limited their ability to adapt effectively to developments in the world energy market and to update their technical know-how.[52] As in most other oil-producing countries, Algerian policymakers have for a long time set internal prices for energy products more with reference to their low cost of production than to their export opportunity cost. The resulting implicit subsidization of energy products has encouraged both consumer demand and industrial use that was already biased toward excessive energy requirements because of the promotion of heavy industries in the central plan and distorted relative prices that favored capital intensity. As a result, Algeria's per capita energy consumption has been several times greater than in neighboring countries without a corresponding difference in per capita income.[53]

Foreign Participation and Evolution of Domestic Pricing Policy

The lack of foreign participation in oil and gas production became particularly costly following the 1986 reverse oil shock. In a major break with the past, the authorities responded by relaxing the legal constraints to foreign participation in the hydrocar-

---

[48]Société Nationale pour le Transport et la Commercialisation des Hydrocarbures.

[49]Power generation was the responsibility of another parastatal, Sonelgaz.

[50]The chronology of discoveries as reported in A. Benbitour, *L'expérience álgérienne de développement*, 1992, is 80 percent before 1962, 11 percent in 1963–73, 4 percent in 1974–79, and 5 percent in 1980–87.

[51]Naftal received the responsibility to manage oil refining and domestic distribution of petroleum products, including liquid petroleum gas. Eight new companies were created for special purposes (geophysical research, drilling, and petroleum engineering). Three enterprises were formed for civil works and pipeline construction and three others to produce fertilizers, petrochemicals, plastics, and rubber. Another entity was created for sea transport of hydrocarbon and chemical products. Finally, in 1987, Naftal was itself restructured when its refining activities spun off to a new enterprise, Naftec.

[52]This is in part reflected in the slowdown in drilling activities, which fell from about 100,000 meters a year on average in the late 1970s to 75,000 meters in the first half of the 1980s.

[53]Algeria's per capita energy consumption is over 1 ton of oil equivalent a year, about twice that of Tunisia and four times that of Morocco.

APPENDIX I

bon sector and by adopting a more efficient domestic energy pricing policy.

The petroleum code established by the 1986 hydrocarbon law allowed foreign participation in oil exploration, under the terms of concession agreements, service contracts, or production-sharing contracts. For the first time, foreign companies were permitted to repatriate their profits. Nevertheless, the government's right to acquire a majority interest in any joint venture was maintained. The 1991 amendments to the 1986 law extended some of these provisions to joint ventures in oil production and in the development and exploitation of gas fields. Moreover, foreign companies were granted fiscal status in Algeria, enabling them to avoid double taxation, and Sonatrach's transportation monopoly was terminated.

At the same time, the authorities also introduced a new policy regarding the pricing of energy products for domestic consumption. This policy has aimed at bringing prices of most energy products in line with their economic costs. Besides improving allocative efficiency, this new approach has encouraged energy conservation and substitution of natural gas for petroleum products. It has also improved the financial situation of local refineries and distributors as well as their contribution to the government's budget. The first major adjustments to domestic energy prices occurred in 1989 and 1992. After a pause, this policy acquired a new momentum in the context of the 1994/95 IMF-supported program. From April 1994 to March 1995, domestic prices of energy products increased on average by 75 percent and the implicit subsidy—reflected in the difference between the domestic price and the true opportunity cost implied by export prices—was reduced to about 10 percent of their economic costs.[54] Energy prices were raised further in 1995 to eliminate the subsidy, and further price adjustments took place to offset the world oil price increases that occurred in 1996–97.

Production and Exports

Reflecting the diversification strategy pursued by Sonatrach, the product mix has evolved through time, with the share of crude oil declining at first in favor of refined products, and later, in favor of gas. This shift in the product mix started in the 1970s and became more pronounced as a result of investment efforts since the late 1980s, particularly those aimed at intensifying the exploitation of Algeria's considerable gas potential (see Figure 19).

At independence, natural gas resources were still underexploited and hydrocarbon production consisted almost exclusively of crude oil. Crude oil output fell steadily, however, during the first half of the 1980s because of the gradual depletion of some fields, inadequate secondary recoveries, and the constraint represented by OPEC quotas. By 1984, crude oil production stood at 64 percent of its 1979 level (Table A1).

Refining capacity remained limited during the 1960s, but began to expand during the 1970s, reaching its peak in 1981, when the coming-on-line of the Skikda plant brought overall capacity from 150,000 barrels a day to 475,000 barrels a day or about 60 percent of 1996 crude oil production. On the one hand, production of refined products increased more than threefold between 1979 and 1984. Since then, the margins on refined products have been steadily eroded as a result of new entries of efficient suppliers in the world market and increasing production costs to meet higher environmental standards. As a result, the additional refinery constructions contemplated in the early 1980s have been abandoned and there are no plans for further capacity expansion in the future. On the other hand, rapidly growing domestic demand reduced the amount of refined products (or crude oil) available for exports. This was particularly evident through the 1970s when domestic consumption of refined petroleum products (3.9 million tons in 1979) absorbed most of the production (5.4 million tons).

The exploitation of natural gas became significant in the mid-1970s, when the quadrupling of oil prices made it profitable to build Algeria's second and largest gas liquefaction complex and invest in additional expensive gas tankers. Another crucial development in the sector occurred in 1983 with the completion of the trans-Med pipeline to Italy, which marked the beginning of a marketing strategy seeking to exploit vast European potential demand for cleaner sources of energy. Total gas production (after reinjection) increased by more than 25 percent between 1979 and 1984.

At the end of the 1970s, liquefied petroleum gas and condensate output amounted to about 10 percent of crude oil production. This share increased to more than 40 percent by 1984 mainly as a result of both the higher production of refined petroleum products and the increased extraction of natural gas, the two energy sources with which liquefied petroleum gas is a joint product.

The changing composition of exports mirrored the increased importance of refined petroleum products and gas in hydrocarbon production. The share of petroleum products in total export receipts declined from 94 percent in 1979 to 78 percent in 1984, with a corresponding increase in the contribution of gas products from 6 percent to 22 percent. This rise in gas exports would have been even more pronounced if Sonatrach's gas marketing and pricing strategy had not resulted in the loss of significant markets in Germany, the United

---

[54]This implicit subsidy was financed through lower revenue transfers from the oil refineries to the treasury.

Appendix I

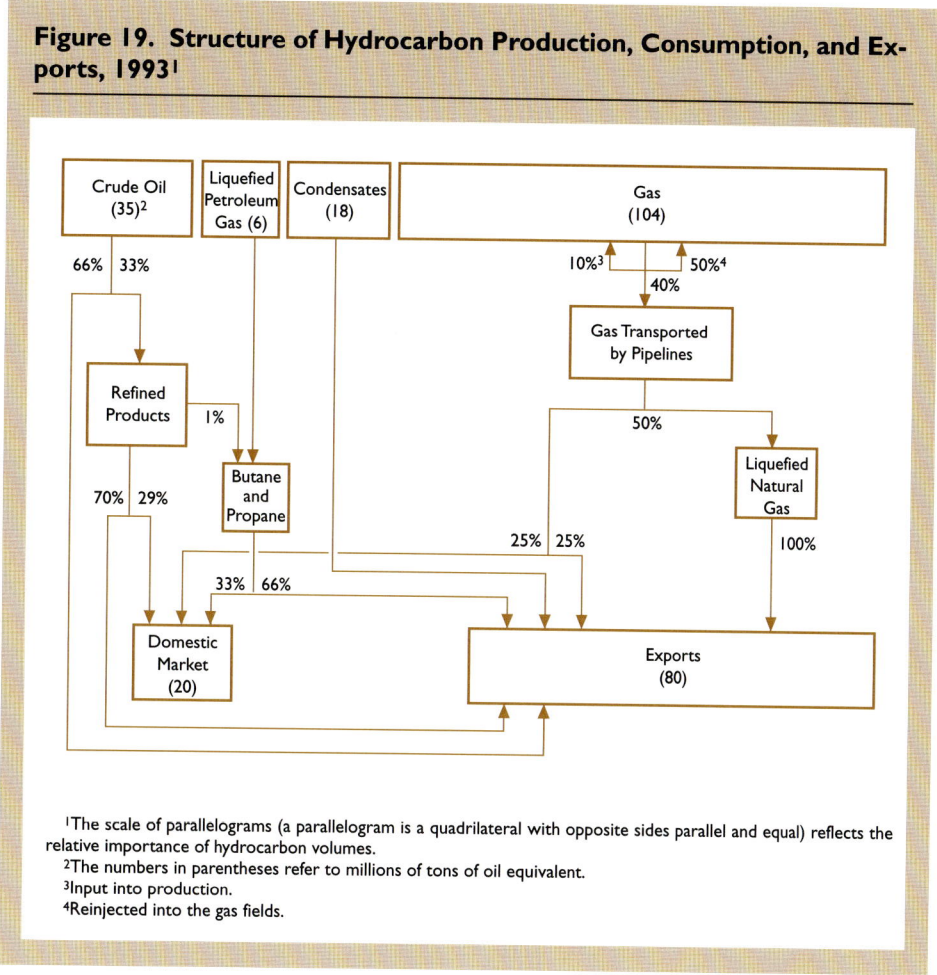

Figure 19. Structure of Hydrocarbon Production, Consumption, and Exports, 1993[1]

[1] The scale of parallelograms (a parallelogram is a quadrilateral with opposite sides parallel and equal) reflects the relative importance of hydrocarbon volumes.
[2] The numbers in parentheses refer to millions of tons of oil equivalent.
[3] Input into production.
[4] Reinjected into the gas fields.

States, and the United Kingdom, and the subsequent underutilization of liquefied natural gas capacity.[55] Within the group of petroleum products, the volume of crude oil exported fell by two-thirds during this period, while exports of condensate and refined products increased almost fourfold.

The trend in favor of gas production and exports has continued since the mid-1980s. By 1997, the share of gas products in total export receipts had increased to 34 percent, with a corresponding decline in the contribution of petroleum products to 66 percent. (See Table A2 and Figure 19.) Three factors contributed to this evolution. First, gas production and exports more than doubled between 1984 and 1997 as a result of further increases in gas liquefaction capacity and in the throughput volume of pipeline capacity, particularly in 1996 and 1997. Second, the growth of crude oil output has been constrained by an insufficient use of appropriate recovery techniques. Third, increases in domestic consumption of refined petroleum products, in the context of unchanged production levels, have reduced exports of refined petroleum products.

Recent Investments and Medium-Term Prospects

In the context of opening up Algeria's exploration and production of hydrocarbons to foreign participation, a major investment plan was launched in the early 1990s with foreign partners to address four main concerns. First, considering the gradual decline in oil output, there was a need for more exploration activity, particularly in the vast sedimentary basins of the western and southwestern parts of the country

---

[55] In 1979, Sonatrach attempted to modify the price formula in existing contracts. In the course of negotiations, two previous customers (El Paso of the United States and British Gas) terminated their contracts with Algeria. In addition, the American company Panhandle later suspended its purchases of Algerian liquefied natural gas while Distrigas of Boston was forced into liquidation.

APPENDIX I

Table A1. Exports of Hydrocarbons

	1987	1988	1989	1990	1991	1992	1993	1994	1995	1996	1997
Crude petroleum											
Value (in millions of U.S. dollars)	1,717.86	1,339.53	1,894.18	2,730.41	2,207.72	2,089.41	2,001.14	1,978.16	2,156.19	3,118.70	2,620.72
Of which:											
Profit repatriation	—	83.00	—	—	—	—	—	—	—	264.09	363.95
Volume (in millions of barrels)	92.63	10.52	102.65	112.27	108.01	104.21	112.74	121.28	122.65	143.79	132.60
(In millions of metric tons)	11.78	16.14	13.01	14.23	13.69	13.29	14.29	15.47	15.64	18.34	16.85
Unit price (in U.S. dollars per barrel)	18.55		18.45	24.32	20.44	20.05	17.75	16.31	17.58	21.69	19.77
Condensate											
Value (in millions of U.S. dollars)	2,382.71	1,743.72	2,534.72	3,548.73	3,220.99	2,928.13	2,607.36	2,188.36	2,374.73	3,025.08	2,833.19
Of which:											
Profit repatriation	—	—	—	—	—	—	—	—	—	51.78	77.24
Volume (in millions of barrels)	139.88	125.80	142.85	145.38	149.12	146.70	146.89	137.29	137.03	142.63	138.88
(In millions of metric tons)	16.03	14.46	16.42	16.71	17.14	16.87	16.80	15.69	15.66	16.30	15.92
Unit price (in U.S. dollars per barrel)	17.03	13.86	17.74	24.41	21.60	19.96	17.75	15.94	17.33	21.21	20.40
Refined petroleum products											
Value (in millions of U.S. dollars)	1,974.80	1,792.48	1,984.80	2,622.24	2,279.82	2,233.17	1,832.37	1,691.93	1,861.44	2,206.15	2,358.47
Volume (in millions of barrels)	106.57	113.78	103.72	104.72	102.79	108.67	100.72	100.23	103.07	97.83	114.58
(In millions of metric tons)	13.49	14.70	13.40	13.53	13.28	14.15	13.11	12.95	13.32	12.64	14.78
Unit price (in U.S. dollars per barrel)	18.53	15.75	19.14	25.04	22.18	20.55	18.19	16.88	18.06	22.55	20.58
Liquefied petroleum gas											
Value (in millions of U.S. dollars)	441.66	407.11	386.15	671.40	779.01	558.05	535.33	475.01	582.91	818.72	1,110.15
Of which:											
Profit repatriation	—	—	—	—	—	—	—	—	—	6.28	38.82
Volume (in millions of barrels)	39.51	41.65	39.90	42.71	41.77	40.99	41.22	40.70	40.82	45.86	67.44
(In millions of metric tons)	3.38	3.56	3.41	3.65	3.57	3.48	3.49	3.47	3.49	3.91	5.72
Unit price (in U.S. dollars per barrel)	11.18	9.77	9.68	15.72	18.65	13.61	12.99	11.67	14.28	17.85	16.46
Liquefied natural gas											
Value (in millions of U.S. dollars)	1,162.00	1,237.38	1,411.88	1,759.76	2,145.86	1,821.57	1,642.70	1,379.69	1,400.95	1,818.26	2,595.91
Volume (in millions of M3 of liquid natural gas)	23.16	25.01	28.79	31.02	31.86	32.66	33.33	29.98	29.11	32.70	43.42
Volume (in billions of M3 of natural gas equivalent)	13.97	15.00	17.27	18.61	19.11	19.59	20.01	18.00	17.43	19.58	26.00
Volume (in billions of British thermal units)	542.05	591.00	680.44	733.23	752.93	771.85	786.25	711.18	686.74	771.45	1,016.16
Unit price (in U.S. dollars per M3 of liquid natural gas)	50.17	49.50	49.04	56.72	67.36	55.77	49.29	46.02	48.13	55.61	59.79
Unit price (in U.S. dollars per million of British thermal units)	2.14	2.13	2.11	2.40	2.85	2.36	2.09	1.94	2.04	2.36	2.55

Appendix I

Natural gas									
Value (in millions of U.S. dollars)	852.44	831.44	883.97	1,015.49	1,342.56	1,218.52	971.19	893.28	1,351.99	1,647.03	2,140.76
Volume (in billions of M3)	11.66	11.14	12.12	11.61	14.50	15.87	14.28	13.64	19.64	21.17	26.36
Volume (in billions of British thermal units)	436.11	438.92	477.53	457.43	571.30	624.88	562.58	507.54	730.80	787.74	987.00
Unit price (in U.S. dollars per M3)	73.10	74.70	72.93	82.59	93.32	73.53	65.10	66.37	69.76	78.85	81.21
Unit price (in U.S. dollars per million of British thermal units)	1.95	1.89	1.85	2.22	2.35	1.95	1.73	1.76	1.85	2.09	2.17
Total hydrocarbon receipts (in millions of U.S. dollars)	8,531.47	7,351.66	9,095.70	12,348.03	11,975.96	10,848.84	9,590.10	8,606.42	9,728.21	12,633.94	1,369.00
					(In percent of total exports)					
Crude petroleum	20.14	18.22	20.83	22.11	18.43	19.26	20.87	22.98	22.16	24.69	19.19
Other	79.86	81.78	79.17	77.89	81.57	80.74	79.13	77.02	77.84	75.31	80.81
Condensate	27.93	23.72	27.87	28.74	26.90	26.99	27.19	25.43	24.41	23.94	20.74
Refined petroleum products	23.15	24.38	21.82	21.24	19.04	20.58	19.11	19.66	19.13	17.46	17.27
Liquefied petroleum gas	5.18	5.54	4.25	5.44	6.50	5.14	5.58	5.52	5.99	6.48	8.13
Liquefied natural gas	13.62	16.83	15.52	14.25	17.92	16.79	17.13	16.03	14.40	14.39	19.01
Natural gas	9.99	11.31	9.72	8.22	11.21	11.23	10.13	10.38	13.90	13.04	15.67

Source: Algerian authorities.

Table A2. Volume of Hydrocarbon Exports

	1987	1988	1989	1990	1991	1992	1993	1994	1995	1996	1997
	(In billions of British thermal units)										
Petroleum and petroleum products											
Crude petroleum	505.3	452.8	560.0	612.4	589.2	568.5	615.0	661.6	669.1	784.4	723.3
Condensate	770.9	693.3	787.3	801.3	821.9	808.5	809.6	756.7	755.2	786.1	765.4
Refined petroleum products	588.8	628.7	573.1	578.6	567.9	600.5	556.5	553.8	569.5	540.6	633.1
Liquefied natural gas	227.2	239.5	229.4	245.6	240.2	235.7	237.0	234.0	234.7	263.7	387.8
Total	2,092.3	2,014.3	2,149.8	2,237.9	2,219.2	2,213.1	2,218.1	2,206.1	2,228.5	2,374.8	2,509.6
Natural gas and liquefied natural gas											
Liquefied natural gas	542.1	591.0	680.4	733.2	752.9	771.9	786.3	711.2	686.7	771.5	1,016.2
Natural gas	436.1	438.9	477.5	457.4	571.3	624.9	562.6	507.4	730.6	787.5	987.0
Total	978.2	1,029.9	1,158.0	1,190.7	1,324.2	1,396.7	1,348.8	1,218.6	1,417.4	1,559.0	2,003.2
Total hydrocarbon trade	3,070.4	3,044.2	3,307.7	3,428.6	3,543.4	3,609.9	3,566.9	3,424.7	3,645.9	3,933.8	4,512.8
	(In percent of total hydrocarbon export volumes)										
Petroleum and petroleum products											
Crude petroleum	16.5	14.9	16.9	17.9	16.6	15.7	17.2	19.3	18.4	19.9	16.0
Condensate	25.1	22.8	23.8	23.4	23.2	22.4	22.7	22.1	20.7	20.0	17.0
Refined petroleum products	19.2	20.7	17.3	16.9	16.0	16.6	15.6	16.2	15.6	13.7	14.0
Liquefied natural gas	7.4	7.9	6.9	7.2	6.8	6.5	6.6	6.8	6.4	6.7	8.6
Total	68.1	66.2	65.0	65.3	62.6	61.3	62.2	64.4	61.1	60.4	55.6
Natural gas and liquefied natural gas											
Liquefied natural gas	17.7	19.4	20.6	21.4	21.2	21.4	22.0	20.8	18.8	19.6	22.5
Natural gas	14.2	14.4	14.4	13.3	16.1	17.3	15.8	14.8	20.0	20.0	21.9
Total	31.9	33.8	35.0	34.7	37.4	38.7	37.8	35.6	38.9	39.6	44.4

Source: Algerian authorities.

that remain largely unexplored,[56] and that account for more than one-half of Algeria's prospective oil and gas acreage. Second, barring significant new discoveries, the yield from proven oil reserves had to be improved through wider adoption of enhanced recovery techniques to maintain current production rates.[57]

Third, Algeria needed to overcome constraints on sales of gas imposed by the existing transportation infrastructure. This called for the construction of new pipelines to less-developed gas fields and to new markets, as well as the expansion of the present network to meet greater prospective domestic and foreign demands. Global demand for gas in recent years has grown rapidly in response to heightened environmental concerns and because of the shift away from nuclear plants to safer, gas-dependent technologies for power generation.[58] Fourth, liquefaction facilities had to be properly maintained and upgraded to prepare Algeria for a likely "deregionalization" of international trade in gas. Liquefied natural gas trade offers a more flexible way to market natural gas and avoids the political risks associated with transportation by pipelines.

Since the passage of the 1986 law on foreign participation in the hydrocarbon sector, Sonatrach has signed over 30 production-sharing and exploration agreements involving a corresponding financial commitment by foreign partners in excess of $1 billion. Negotiations between Sonatrach and foreign firms have not been significantly hampered by the current civil strife, in part because most hydrocarbon activities in Algeria are located in remote areas removed from political unrest. Indeed, over one-half of the aforementioned agreements, worth over $500 million, were concluded with 23 foreign companies since the aggravation of political tensions in early 1992. These have led to significant increases in both oil and gas discoveries, and an expansion in production at existing facilities. Cooperation with foreign partners advanced further in the year to April 1996: Algeria signed the first agreement associating a foreign company (BP) in the development and exploitation of known gas fields (Ain Salah); the first agreement associating a foreign company with the exploitation of a producing oil field was signed; and a contract for the development of the Tin Fouye Tabankort gas and condensate field was awarded to two foreign companies in association with Sonatrach.

Foreign companies were responsible for most of the significant oil discoveries during 1994 and 1995.[59] Approximately 16 hydrocarbon discoveries were made in the course of 1994 and 1995, raising the replacement ratio to greater than one. In other words, Algeria more than replaced its marketed production, keeping the reserves-production ratio at about 35 years. As regards the higher production through enhanced recovery methods, the agreement reached earlier with the American company Arco will lead in three phases to an eventual increase in production by Algeria's second largest oil field (Rhourde El Baguel) from 27,000 barrels a day to 125,000 barrels a day by 1999. The first phase involved the installation of gas injection processors to stem the decline in oil production from the field. The second phase involves the installation of four compressors to boost the gas injection capacity. Finally, by 1999, Arco is to have expanded capacity by drilling new wells and adding new flow lines. This is the first agreement of its kind involving a joint operating company between Sonatrach and a foreign partner. It is expected to establish a model for similar contracts in other oil fields such as the Hassi Messaoud reservoir.

Several of Algeria's foreign investment partners have found new discoveries recently, particularly in the Berkine East field. The government has awarded a provisional exploitation license to Anadarko, in which Sonatrach has part equity, to begin the first phase of an estimated $1 billion development in the Hassi Berkine and Hassi Berkine South fields. These and other new oil discoveries together with investment in enhanced oil recovery projects are expected to raise crude production capacity well above Algeria's prevailing OPEC quota of 750,000 barrels a day. Crude output at the end of 1997 was estimated at over 800,000 barrels a day, but growing capacity could shortly accommodate a quota of about 1.25 million barrels a day. While the government is committed to maintaining quota discipline within OPEC, it hopes to negotiate a new agreement that will allow for increased production.

As regards liquefied petroleum gas, a major project agreed to in 1994 (the "Jumbo liquefied petroleum gas" unit at Arzew) with Japanese construction and financial backing was delayed for some time because of stalled credits to finance equipment and supplies. These were unblocked in 1996 and construction has been under way. This project will help to double butane and propane production capacity

---

[56] Only about 15 percent of Algeria's 1.5 million square kilometers has been prospected for oil and gas. Thus, the country's exploration density is low relative to other oil-producing regions: the number of drills per 1,000 square kilometers is less than 1, compared with 50 in North America, 4.5 in western Europe, and 9 in the states of the former Soviet Union. See A. Benbitour, *L'expérience álgérienne de développement*, 1992.

[57] Secondary recovery methods are used in about 70 percent of Algeria's crude oil production.

[58] See Thomas P. Enger, "The World Market for Natural Gas: Macroeconomic and Financial Implications," IMF Paper on Policy Analysis and Assessment 93/15 (Washington: International Monetary Fund, 1993).

[59] Major participants included Agip of Italy, Spain's Cepsa, PetroCanada, Mobil, and Anadarko of the United States.

by the end of the decade to 8 million tons a year from the current level of 3.5 million tons a year.

On the transportation front, the trans-Med gas line in the eastern part of Algeria, which stretches over 600 miles, has connected Hassi R'Mel to Italy since 1983. It was recently expanded, in collaboration with Italian companies, to increase its maximum annual throughput from 16 billion cubic meters to 24 billion cubic meters. In addition, Sonatrach has been pumping liquefied petroleum gas through its 1,000 kilometer pipeline running from Alrar and other southern fields to Hassi R'Mel.

A second large-scale project—the construction of the 700-mile Maghreb-Europe gas line from Hassi R'Mel to Seville via Morocco—was completed in early 1997 and involved a variety of foreign partners. Natural gas flows started in December 1996, consolidating Algeria's position as the world's fourth largest gas exporter. The Maghreb-Europe gas line will provide throughput capacity of 9.5 billion cubic meters a year and will serve the Moroccan, Portuguese, and Spanish markets. Morocco is not taking gas through the Maghreb-Europe gas line because the power plant projects targeted to use the gas have not yet been commissioned. In the interim, Spain will pay a rent to Morocco for the gas crossing Moroccan territory. This is based on a model developed for the sale of Algerian gas to Italy via the trans-Med pipeline, which crosses Tunisia. In a second phase, the Maghreb-Europe gas line's initial capacity could be doubled with the installation of additional compression stations in Algeria, and further extensions would allow direct supplies to France and Germany. To ensure full use of these two export pipelines, there is a need to connect the gas fields in the southeastern basin (Alrar) with the network node at Hassi R'Mel; foreign partners have already expressed interest in such an undertaking for which Sonatrach is seeking external financing.

As for liquefied natural gas production, Sonatrach completed rehabilitation work on Algeria's three liquefaction plants by the end of 1996. (Work at the fourth plant—Skikda—was delayed but is expected to be completed by 1998.) The renovation was the product of a $1.5 billion program started in 1990, which included substantial input from foreign partners.[60] This program will restore the plants' capacity to their originally targeted level of 30.5 billion cubic meters in late 1998.

The government is trying to promote increased domestic use of natural gas. The state-owned Société Nationale de l'Electricité et du Gaz (Sonelgaz) predicts that Algeria's gas consumption will more than double by 2010. With a further expansion of the distribution network (see below) and the growing demand on the part of power stations, this will translate into an average annual rate of consumption growth of 4.6 percent over the period. Sonelgaz aims to achieve 90 percent penetration of the Algerian market, which will require a further expansion of the gas line network and revitalization of the public gas distribution program.

The expansion of the trans-Med pipeline, the construction of the Maghreb-Europe gas line, and the revamping of the liquefied natural gas facilities will help to boost Algeria's gas exports considerably. Together with new gas production facilities scheduled to come on stream in 1997 and 1998, Algeria should be able to reach its annual target for gas exports of 60 billion cubic meters a year by the end of the decade compared with 32 billion cubic meters a year in 1994 (about 26 million cubic meters a year will be exported in the form of liquefied natural gas). The corresponding sales contracts have already been secured, and expected trends in global demand suggest that a more ambitious export target could be justified.

Foreign partnership will continue to play a central role in the gas sector. The Arzew-based joint venture Helios has commissioned studies that could lead to the construction of a second helium and nitrogen production plant in Algeria, provided sales contracts can be concluded with major clients. Helios already sells its helium output to U.S. and French shareholders, and all of its nitrogen to Sonatrach. To summarize, total production capacity is about 62 billion cubic meters a year, and with the completion of the first phase of the Maghreb-Europe gas line, total export capacity will be 34 cubic meters a year by gas line (10 billion cubic meters a year through the Maghreb-Europe gas line and 24 billion cubic meters a year through trans-Med).

Current volume projections envisage a 20 percent increase in hydrocarbon exports by 2001: this incorporates an increase of roughly 20 percent in both gas and petroleum products exported. Owing to the downward revision in medium-term oil prices, this would increase annual export receipts by 11 percent over the next four years. Western Europe absorbs more than 80 percent of Algeria's total exports of crude oil. Germany became the biggest buyer of Algerian crude in 1993 and 1994 ahead of France, Italy, the United States, and the United Kingdom. Algeria's main market for natural gas is western Europe, which absorbs over 30 billion cubic meters a year. Moreover, this market is expected to face an estimated annual gas shortfall of 33 billion cubic meters a year by 2000. Sonatrach hopes to cover up to 40 percent of that deficit in view of Algeria's particular advantages, such as proximity, the size of its gas reserves, a favorable investment regime, and the

---

[60]American, French, and Belgian companies provided technical expertise, while most of the financing came from export credit agencies of Canada, France, Japan, the United Kingdom, and the United States.

existence of an established transport infrastructure whose capacity is being increased. In addition, Sonatrach is targeting other markets, including neighboring African countries and North America.

Algeria's energy production has doubled every 10 years since 1971, and according to Sonatrach officials, it could double again by 2006 if exploration and development activities continue at the prevailing pace. Successful implementation of the new investment strategy will place Algeria in a good position to take advantage of the favorable demand prospects for its energy products. To fulfill export projections, Algeria's hydrocarbon sector will have to keep displaying enough technical and managerial flexibility to cope with challenges posed by an increasingly competitive marketplace. This will require both fostering foreign participation and further restructuring of the industry, including the privatization of some elements of the Sonatrach group.

Implications for Macroeconomic Policy

The presence of a large natural resource sector has been an important element in shaping the structure and management of the Algerian economy. For instance, it weakened incentives to develop tradables production outside the hydrocarbon sector, and influenced the design of the tax structure by reducing the necessity to develop alternative revenue sources.

Indeed, Algeria's dependence on hydrocarbon revenue as the major source of foreign exchange also has important macroeconomic implications since the volatility of international oil prices has translated into the volatility of important macroeconomic aggregates. Movements in international energy prices have generated corresponding variations in the value of exports, government revenues, and the availability of foreign exchange. There has been, for example, a strong correlation between changes in international oil prices and real GDP growth, which seems to have become even more pronounced in the 1990s.

Links between growth and other aggregates, on the one hand, and international oil prices, on the other hand, have operated through a number of channels. With respect to the impact on growth, oil price variations have affected both demand and supply. In the face of adverse price (or output) developments in the hydrocarbon sector, negative wealth effects are likely to have reduced consumption demand, reinforced by a compression of government expenditure and lower investment outlays. In addition, in the early 1990s, the defense of the exchange rate peg required periodic intensification of rationing of foreign exchange or increased recourse to foreign borrowing. Formal or informal foreign exchange rationing affected supply, by reducing access to imported inputs (and distorting their selection), thereby leading to a fall in capacity utilization and a deterioration of capital equipment owing to shortages of spare parts. For instance, as Algeria's access to external credit weakened in the late 1980s, formal payment restrictions were introduced to repress excess demand for foreign exchange, a development that may explain the more pronounced link between oil prices and growth in recent years.

Through the budget's dependence on revenue from the oil sector, fluctuations in oil prices had important direct implications for public expenditure management. Favorable oil prices were often seen as signaling permanent increases in income, and triggered higher levels of public expenditure that were difficult to reduce once the boom had proven only temporary. For example, following the reverse oil shock of 1986, budgetary revenue fell sharply from 38 percent of GDP during 1981–85 to 28 percent of GDP during 1986–90. As public expenditure—mostly capital expenditure—could only be reduced by about 5 percentage points of GDP, the fiscal deficit shifted from an average surplus of 3.5 percent of GDP in 1981–85 to a deficit of about 2.7 percent of GDP in 1986–90.

Over the coming years, the relative importance of the hydrocarbon sector is unlikely to change substantially. Nonhydrocarbon activity is expected to benefit eventually from the impact of liberalization and a growing private sector, notably in agriculture, industry, and construction in response to the strong demand for housing, although in the near term, output may be sluggish as divestment of state industries leads to contraction in employment. The continued impact of the real exchange rate depreciation of 1994–95 (and the maintenance of a competitive exchange rate) is also likely to stimulate tradables production outside the hydrocarbon sector and, over time, reduce somewhat the relative importance of hydrocarbon exports. Nonetheless, under baseline projections, hydrocarbon exports are still likely to account for about 85 percent of total exports by 2005.

Under this outlook, Algeria's vulnerability to fluctuations in international energy prices will decline only modestly over the next years. For example, hydrocarbon exports would decline by about $700 million annually for every $1 per barrel decline in the price of oil. Real GDP growth would be lower, the external debt/GDP ratio would decline only marginally (and could rise depending on the magnitude of the oil price drop), and current account deficits would be larger. Since borrowing from abroad to maintain the same level of absorption may be inappropriate, Algeria would have to respond to such a shock with adjustment measures, including further fiscal tightening and possibly exchange rate depreciation to reduce imports and accelerate the development of exports outside the hydrocarbon sector. More notably, structural reforms would have to be seriously accelerated.

By contrast, higher oil prices would raise different policy issues and would under current circumstances warrant an asymmetric policy response. In particular, if the higher revenue from the hydrocarbon sector were to be used to reduce public debt rather than finance higher spending, and if pressure toward a real exchange rate appreciation were to be resisted, it would reduce Algeria's vulnerability to future adverse price shocks, strengthen the current account, and further alleviate the debt-service burden, as the external debt/GDP ratio would decline more rapidly. Indeed, these trends began to materialize in 1996.

In any event, the shift to a managed float of the exchange rate in 1994–95 changed the nature of the mechanism transmitting changes in oil prices to macroeconomic aggregates. Most importantly, continued exchange rate flexibility will protect Algeria from some of the destabilizing effects of energy price volatility. A deepening in the domestic financial and foreign exchange markets and their integration into global financial markets would further increase such protection. For example, adverse oil shocks that are perceived by the market as temporary would cause less pressure on the exchange rate, and the temporary widening of the current account deficit would be more readily financed from abroad, thereby smoothing out the path of aggregate income and absorption. By contrast, market perception of a more permanent adverse oil shock would result in strong pressure on the exchange rate, signaling the need for a real depreciation to channel resources into the tradables sector and a tightening in demand management policies. Exchange rate flexibility would avoid the need for nominal wage and price deflation that may be difficult to implement in Algeria given the strength of labor in the sociopolitical landscape. Stabilizing output and relative prices in the face of shocks perceived by markets as temporary, while quickly adjusting to permanent shocks, will have the additional effect of supporting investment by reducing the risk premium that agents, faced with uncertainty about relative sectoral profitability, will attach to the required rate of return.

To conclude, continued predominance of the hydrocarbon sector in Algeria's economy means policymakers will have to continue to respect the power of energy price fluctuations on the domestic economy. This influence will have to be taken into account in the formulation of economic policy, with a view to minimizing the adverse impact of volatility in international energy markets while implementing policies that help diversify the Algerian economy over the longer term. In this respect, employment creation will have to come almost exclusively from the nonhydrocarbon sector. Indeed, the social and economic costs of unemployment—the biggest challenge currently facing policymakers—point to the urgency behind the authorities' efforts to invigorate the nonhydrocarbon private sector with their program of structural reform and privatization.

Appendix II Dynamics of Unemployment

This appendix aims at providing an assessment of employment developments in the context of different growth scenarios using a simple growth/employment framework.[61] The projections in this appendix assume that participation (as a percentage of the population) continues to rise through 2010 in line with recent trends, while population growth continues to slow. On a net basis, there would be about 250,000 new entrants to the Algerian labor market each year.

To establish a link between output growth and the demand for labor, assumptions need to be made regarding the elasticity of employment to growth. Past developments provide little guidance, as recruitment policies in the dominant public sector reflected political and social concerns rather than efficiency considerations. Thus, while real GDP remained virtually flat, total employment expanded by 34 percent between 1985 and 1995, from 4.06 million to 5.44 million; of this, government employment rose from 900,000 to 1.29 million. Sectoral elasticities have also fluctuated widely for 1991–95. In agriculture, the most dynamic and most labor-intensive sector, the elasticity of employment to GDP growth was about 0.6. In the rest of the economy, the average elasticity during

---

[61]The analysis in this appendix draws on the study of Klaus Enders, "Labor Market Prospects in Algeria" (unpublished mimeo: International Monetary Fund, 1996). Assuming that Algeria's GDP can be summarized by a simple Cobb-Douglas production function $Y = AL^\alpha K^{1-\alpha} = ALk^{1-\alpha}$, where Y is real GDP, L is employment, K is the capital stock, $k = K/L$ is the capital stock per worker, A is a measure of total factor productivity (TFP), and α is the share of labor income in GDP, and denoting percentage change in a variable by a hat (^), and thus,

$$\hat{Y} = \hat{L} + \hat{A} + (1-\alpha)\hat{k} = \hat{L} + \hat{y}$$

with $y = Y/L$ total labor productivity, the partial elasticity of employment with respect to output (i.e., given A and k) is then equal to one. The global elasticity referred to in the scenarios may be different if there are annual TFP gains ($\hat{A} > 0$) and/or if capital endowment per worker k changes. Clearly, Algeria's structural reforms should aim at raising TFP, which by itself would reduce demand for labor for any given output growth rate. In particular, reform of the public enterprise sector and labor shedding will raise A. At the same time, wage restraint would help lowering capital intensity (k); policies geared toward stimulating housing production (where the sectoral k is likely low) would lower the economy's overall capital intensity; in agriculture, where land supply is more or less fixed, expansion of output may continue to require growth in employment; and in industrial sectors with currently low rates of capacity utilization, expansion of production would also result in employment gains without much additional investment.

Figure 20. Unemployment Rates Under Low- and High-Growth Scenarios

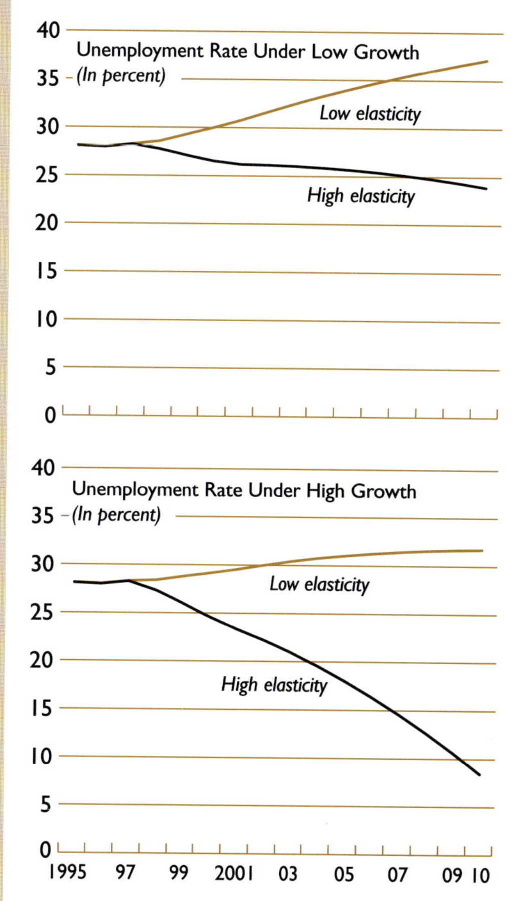

Source: IMF staff estimates and projections.

APPENDIX II

Table A3. Employment Prospects: High-Growth Scenario

	Estimates			Projections					
	1995	1996	1997	1998	1999	2000	2001	2002	2003
	(In percent)								
Population growth rate	2.1	2.0	2.0	1.9	1.9	1.8	1.8	1.7	1.7
Rural	0.4	0.3	0.3	0.2	0.2	0.2	0.3	0.3	0.3
Urban	3.5	3.4	3.3	3.2	3.1	2.9	2.8	2.7	2.6
Labor force growth	11.0	3.3	2.2	3.0	3.0	2.9	2.9	2.8	2.8
Participation (percent of total population)	27.0	27.3	27.4	27.7	28.0	28.3	28.6	28.9	29.2
Real GDP growth[1]	4.3	4.6	1.0	5.5	5.0	5.0	4.7	4.4	4.4
Agriculture	15.1	21.3	−13.5	11.4	5.8	5.8	5.8	5.8	5.8
Government	3.4	3.0	2.5	2.5	2.5	2.5	2.5	2.5	2.5
Other sectors	2.8	2.3	3.3	5.2	5.4	5.4	5.0	4.5	4.5
High elasticities scenario									
Assumed sectoral elasticities									
Agriculture	0.4	0.3	0.1	0.5	1.0	1.0	1.0	1.0	1.0
Government	2.0	0.9	0.5	0.5	0.5	0.5	0.5	0.5	0.5
Other sectors	1.7	1.2	0.9	1.0	1.1	1.1	1.1	1.1	1.1
	(In millions; unless otherwise indicated)								
Total employment	5.4	5.6	5.7	6.0	6.3	6.6	6.9	7.2	7.5
Agriculture	1.1	1.2	1.1	1.2	1.3	1.4	1.4	1.5	1.6
Government	1.3	1.3	1.3	1.4	1.4	1.4	1.4	1.4	1.4
Other sectors	3.1	3.1	3.2	3.4	3.6	3.8	4.0	4.2	4.4
Unemployment rate[1]	28.1	28.0	28.3	27.3	26.0	24.6	23.3	22.2	21.0
Unemployment	2.1	2.2	2.3	2.2	2.2	2.1	2.1	2.0	2.0
Low elasticities scenario									
Assumed sectoral elasticities									
Agriculture	0.4	0.3	0.1	0.5	0.5	0.5	0.5	0.5	0.5
Government	2.0	0.9	0.5	0.5	0.5	0.5	0.5	0.5	0.5
Other sectors	1.7	1.2	0.9	0.5	0.5	0.5	0.5	0.5	0.5
	(In millions; unless otherwise indicated)								
Total employment	5.4	5.6	5.7	5.8	5.9	6.1	6.2	6.3	6.5
Agriculture	1.1	1.2	1.1	1.2	1.2	1.2	1.3	1.4	1.4
Government	1.3	1.3	1.3	1.4	1.4	1.4	1.4	1.4	1.4
Other sectors	3.1	3.1	3.2	3.3	3.4	3.5	3.6	3.7	3.8
Unemployment rate[2]	28.1	28.0	28.3	28.4	28.7	29.1	29.5	30.0	30.4
Unemployment	2.1	2.2	2.3	2.3	2.4	2.5	2.6	2.8	2.9

Source: Data provided by the Algerian authorities; and IMF staff estimates and projections.
[1]At factor costs.
[2]In percent.

1991–95 was high but negative, as public enterprises continued to recruit despite stagnating or declining output.

To indicate a broad range of possible outcomes, two scenarios have been developed (Tables A3 and A4, and Figure 20). In the first scenario, Low Growth, annual growth of real GDP during 1998–2010 averages about 3.2 percent, with manufacturing growth averaging 2 percent. In the second scenario, High Growth, higher annual growth in manufacturing (5.7 percent on average) results in annual GDP growth of about 5 percent on average during the same period. In both scenarios, government employment slows, as the authorities reduce net recruitment even while upgrading the qualification levels of the civil service. For each scenario, two

Appendix II

Table A4. Employment Prospects: Low-Growth Scenario

	Estimates			Projections					
	1995	1996	1997	1998	1999	2000	2001	2002	2003
	(In percent)								
Population growth rate	2.1	2.0	2.0	1.9	1.9	1.8	1.8	1.7	1.7
Rural	0.4	0.3	0.3	0.2	0.2	0.2	0.3	0.3	0.3
Urban	3.5	3.4	3.3	3.2	3.1	2.9	2.8	2.7	2.6
Labor force growth	11.0	3.3	2.2	3.0	3.0	2.9	2.9	2.8	2.8
Participation (percent of total population)	27.0	27.3	27.4	27.7	28.0	28.3	28.6	28.9	29.2
Real GDP growth[1]	4.3	4.6	1.0	4.7	4.0	3.8	3.3	2.8	2.8
Agriculture	15.1	21.3	−13.5	11.4	5.0	5.0	5.0	5.0	5.0
Government	3.4	3.0	2.5	2.5	2.5	2.5	2.5	2.5	2.5
Other sectors	2.8	2.3	3.3	4.0	4.1	3.9	3.2	2.5	2.5
High elasticities scenario									
Assumed sectoral elasticities									
Agriculture	0.4	0.3	0.1	0.5	1.0	1.0	1.0	1.0	1.0
Government	2.0	0.9	0.5	0.5	0.5	0.5	0.5	0.5	0.5
Other sectors	1.7	1.2	0.9	1.0	1.1	1.1	1.1	1.1	1.1
	(In millions; unless otherwise indicated)								
Total employment	5.4	5.6	5.7	5.9	6.2	6.4	6.6	6.8	7.0
Agriculture	1.1	1.2	1.1	1.2	1.3	1.3	1.4	1.5	1.5
Government	1.3	1.3	1.3	1.4	1.4	1.4	1.4	1.4	1.4
Other sectors	3.1	3.1	3.2	3.4	3.5	3.7	3.8	3.9	4.0
Unemployment rate[1]	28.1	28.0	28.3	27.8	27.1	26.6	26.2	26.2	26.1
Unemployment	2.1	2.2	2.3	2.3	2.3	2.3	2.4	2.4	2.5
Low elasticities scenario									
Assumed sectoral elasticities									
Agriculture	0.4	0.3	0.1	0.5	0.5	0.5	0.5	0.5	0.5
Government	2.0	0.9	0.5	0.5	0.5	0.5	0.5	0.5	0.5
Other sectors	1.7	1.2	0.9	0.5	0.5	0.5	0.5	0.5	0.5
	(In millions; unless otherwise indicated)								
Total employment	5.4	5.6	5.7	5.9	6.0	6.1	6.2	6.3	6.4
Agriculture	1.1	1.2	1.1	1.2	1.2	1.3	1.3	1.3	1.4
Government	1.3	1.3	1.3	1.4	1.4	1.4	1.4	1.4	1.4
Other sectors	3.1	3.1	3.2	3.3	3.3	3.4	3.5	3.5	1.6
Unemployment rate[2]	28.1	28.0	28.3	28.6	29.3	30.0	30.8	31.6	32.5
Unemployment	2.1	2.2	2.3	2.4	2.5	2.6	2.8	2.9	3.1

Source: Data provided by the Algerian authorities; and IMF staff estimates and projections.
[1] At factor costs.
[2] In percent.

sets of assumptions regarding the sectoral employment/output elasticities outside the government sector are examined. Under a pessimistic assumption, sectoral elasticities remain low at about 0.5, broadly in line with elasticities observed in other countries, while under an "optimistic" assumption, the total elasticity remains constant at about one.

Under the low-growth scenario, and assuming high elasticities of employment/output creation, unemployment would only fall to 26 percent by 2001 and 23 percent by 2010, with 2.9 million jobs created during 1998–2010. Making the pessimistic assumptions on elasticities, unemployment would rise rapidly to about 31 percent by 2001 and about 37 percent by 2010. Under the high-growth scenario, and assuming high elasticities, about 1.2 million jobs would be created between 1998 and 2001, and another 3.5 million by 2010; unemployment would fall to 23 percent by 2001 and to about 8 percent by 2010. Assuming low elasticities, high growth would be insufficient to reduce unemployment, which would gradually rise to 32 percent by 2010, even while a total number of 2.1 million jobs are created between 1998 and 2010. As discussed above, the high elasticity outcomes would become more likely with further reforms of the labor market and a continued restrained incomes policy to make economic growth more labor intensive. Strong growth in the construction sector to alleviate the housing shortage, in particular, could contribute substantially to further raising the labor-intensity of GDP. At the same time, strong and credible reform policies may help Algeria to achieve growth above 6 percent, which, even in the presence of relatively low elasticities, would help generate faster employment gains.

Recent Occasional Papers of the International Monetary Fund

165. Algeria: Stabilization and Transition to the Market, by Karim Nashashibi, Patricia Alonso-Gamo, Stefania Bazzoni, Alain Féler, Nicole Laframboise, and Sebastian Paris Horvitz. 1998.

164. MULTIMOD Mark III: The Core Dynamic and Steady-State Model, by Douglas Laxton, Peter Isard, Hamid Faruqee, Eswar Prasad, and Bart Turtelboom. 1998.

163. Egypt: Beyond Stabilization, Toward a Dynamic Market Economy, by a staff team led by Howard Handy. 1998.

162. Fiscal Policy Rules, by George Kopits and Steven Symansky. 1998.

161. The Nordic Banking Crises: Pitfalls in Financial Liberalization? by Burkhard Dress and Ceyla Pazarbaşıoğlu. 1998.

160. Fiscal Reform in Low-Income Countries: Experience Under IMF-Supported Programs, by a staff team led by George T. Abed and comprising Liam Ebrill, Sanjeev Gupta, Benedict Clements, Ronald McMorran, Anthony Pellechio, Jerald Schiff, and Marijn Verhoeven. 1998.

159. Hungary: Economic Policies for Sustainable Growth, Carlo Cottarelli, Thomas Krueger, Reza Moghadam, Perry Perone, Edgardo Ruggiero, and Rachel van Elkan. 1998.

158. Transparency in Government Operations, by George Kopits and Jon Craig. 1998.

157. Central Bank Reforms in the Baltics, Russia, and the Other Countries of the Former Soviet Union, by a staff team led by Malcolm Knight and comprising Susana Almuiña, John Dalton, Inci Otker, Ceyla Pazarbaşıoğlu, Arne B. Petersen, Peter Quirk, Nicholas M. Roberts, Gabriel Sensenbrenner, and Jan Willem van der Vossen. 1997.

156. The ESAF at Ten Years: Economic Adjustment and Reform in Low-Income Countries, by the staff of the International Monetary Fund. 1997.

155. Fiscal Policy Issues During the Transition in Russia, by Augusto Lopez-Claros and Sergei V. Alexashenko. 1998.

154. Credibility Without Rules? Monetary Frameworks in the Post–Bretton Woods Era, by Carlo Cottarelli and Curzio Giannini. 1997.

153. Pension Regimes and Saving, by G.A. Mackenzie, Philip Gerson, and Alfredo Cuevas. 1997.

152. Hong Kong, China: Growth, Structural Change, and Economic Stability During the Transition, by John Dodsworth and Dubravko Mihaljek. 1997.

151. Currency Board Arrangements: Issues and Experiences, by a staff team led by Tomás J.T. Baliño and Charles Enoch. 1997.

150. Kuwait: From Reconstruction to Accumulation for Future Generations, by Nigel Andrew Chalk, Mohamed A. El-Erian, Susan J. Fennell, Alexei P. Kireyev, and John F. Wilson. 1997.

149. The Composition of Fiscal Adjustment and Growth: Lessons from Fiscal Reforms in Eight Economies, by G.A. Mackenzie, David W.H. Orsmond, and Philip R. Gerson. 1997.

148. Nigeria: Experience with Structural Adjustment, by Gary Moser, Scott Rogers, and Reinold van Til, with Robin Kibuka and Inutu Lukonga. 1997.

147. Aging Populations and Public Pension Schemes, by Sheetal K. Chand and Albert Jaeger. 1996.

146. Thailand: The Road to Sustained Growth, by Kalpana Kochhar, Louis Dicks-Mireaux, Balazs Horvath, Mauro Mecagni, Erik Offerdal, and Jianping Zhou. 1996.

145. Exchange Rate Movements and Their Impact on Trade and Investment in the APEC Region, by Takatoshi Ito, Peter Isard, Steven Symansky, and Tamim Bayoumi. 1996.

144. National Bank of Poland: The Road to Indirect Instruments, by Piero Ugolini. 1996.

143. Adjustment for Growth: The African Experience, by Michael T. Hadjimichael, Michael Nowak, Robert Sharer, and Amor Tahari. 1996.

142. Quasi-Fiscal Operations of Public Financial Institutions, by G.A. Mackenzie and Peter Stella. 1996.

OCCASIONAL PAPERS

141. Monetary and Exchange System Reforms in China: An Experiment in Gradualism, by Hassanali Mehran, Marc Quintyn, Tom Nordman, and Bernard Laurens. 1996.

140. Government Reform in New Zealand, by Graham C. Scott. 1996.

139. Reinvigorating Growth in Developing Countries: Lessons from Adjustment Policies in Eight Economies, by David Goldsbrough, Sharmini Coorey, Louis Dicks-Mireaux, Balazs Horvath, Kalpana Kochhar, Mauro Mecagni, Erik Offerdal, and Jianping Zhou. 1996.

138. Aftermath of the CFA Franc Devaluation, by Jean A.P. Clément, with Johannes Mueller, Stéphane Cossé, and Jean Le Dem. 1996.

137. The Lao People's Democratic Republic: Systemic Transformation and Adjustment, edited by Ichiro Otani and Chi Do Pham. 1996.

136. Jordan: Strategy for Adjustment and Growth, edited by Edouard Maciejewski and Ahsan Mansur. 1996.

135. Vietnam: Transition to a Market Economy, by John R. Dodsworth, Erich Spitäller, Michael Braulke, Keon Hyok Lee, Kenneth Miranda, Christian Mulder, Hisanobu Shishido, and Krishna Srinivasan. 1996.

134. India: Economic Reform and Growth, by Ajai Chopra, Charles Collyns, Richard Hemming, and Karen Parker with Woosik Chu and Oliver Fratzscher. 1995.

133. Policy Experiences and Issues in the Baltics, Russia, and Other Countries of the Former Soviet Union, edited by Daniel A. Citrin and Ashok K. Lahiri. 1995.

132. Financial Fragilities in Latin America: The 1980s and 1990s, by Liliana Rojas-Suárez and Steven R. Weisbrod. 1995.

131. Capital Account Convertibility: Review of Experience and Implications for IMF Policies, by staff teams headed by Peter J. Quirk and Owen Evans. 1995.

130. Challenges to the Swedish Welfare State, by Desmond Lachman, Adam Bennett, John H. Green, Robert Hagemann, and Ramana Ramaswamy. 1995.

129. IMF Conditionality: Experience Under Stand-By and Extended Arrangements. Part II: Background Papers. Susan Schadler, Editor, with Adam Bennett, Maria Carkovic, Louis Dicks-Mireaux, Mauro Mecagni, James H.J. Morsink, and Miguel A. Savastano. 1995.

128. IMF Conditionality: Experience Under Stand-By and Extended Arrangements. Part I: Key Issues and Findings, by Susan Schadler, Adam Bennett, Maria Carkovic, Louis Dicks-Mireaux, Mauro Mecagni, James H.J. Morsink, and Miguel A. Savastano. 1995.

127. Road Maps of the Transition: The Baltics, the Czech Republic, Hungary, and Russia, by Biswajit Banerjee, Vincent Koen, Thomas Krueger, Mark S. Lutz, Michael Marrese, and Tapio O. Saavalainen. 1995.

126. The Adoption of Indirect Instruments of Monetary Policy, by a staff team headed by William E. Alexander, Tomás J.T. Baliño, and Charles Enoch. 1995.

125. United Germany: The First Five Years—Performance and Policy Issues, by Robert Corker, Robert A. Feldman, Karl Habermeier, Hari Vittas, and Tessa van der Willigen. 1995.

124. Saving Behavior and the Asset Price "Bubble" in Japan: Analytical Studies, edited by Ulrich Baumgartner and Guy Meredith. 1995.

123. Comprehensive Tax Reform: The Colombian Experience, edited by Parthasarathi Shome. 1995.

122. Capital Flows in the APEC Region, edited by Mohsin S. Khan and Carmen M. Reinhart. 1995.

121. Uganda: Adjustment with Growth, 1987–94, by Robert L. Sharer, Hema R. De Zoysa, and Calvin A. McDonald. 1995.

120. Economic Dislocation and Recovery in Lebanon, by Sena Eken, Paul Cashin, S. Nuri Erbas, Jose Martelino, and Adnan Mazarei. 1995.

119. Singapore: A Case Study in Rapid Development, edited by Kenneth Bercuson with a staff team comprising Robert G. Carling, Aasim M. Husain, Thomas Rumbaugh, and Rachel van Elkan. 1995.

Note: For information on the title and availability of Occasional Papers not listed, please consult the IMF Publications Catalog or contact IMF Publication Services.